"Dan Darling offer [...] community in an age [...] —*Russell D. Moore*, d [...]

"Daniel Darling is a s[...] reading."
—*Jerry B. Jenkins*, coauthor of the "Left Behind" series

"Daniel Darling shows us how practical prayer can be in the twenty-first century. Reading this book can reboot your prayer life and open a high-speed connection with God."
—*Ray Pritchard*, president, Keep Believing Ministries; and author of An Anchor for the Soul, Man of Honor, and The ABC's of Wisdom

"If I had written an appropriate endorsement for an earlier generation, I would have used words like super, groovy, neat, and perhaps even it rocks. Dan Darling hits exactly the right tone for this generation; therefore, I'd say it's awesome and so there."
—*Cecil Murphey*, coauthor of 90 Minutes in Heaven

"Many question whether the ancient truths of Christianity connect with the instant expectations of postmodern culture. Darling answers with both a biblical and applicable approach for those in doubt. *iFaith* is the perfect response for the digital generation. Read it, live it, and forward it to a friend!"
—*Dillon Burroughs*, best-selling writer of more than 26 books

"Each chapter includes fresh insight and practical pointers that will enrich your walk with Christ."
—*Charles Stone*, senior pastor at Ginger Creek Community Church

"*iFaith: Connecting with God in the 21st Century* is a must-read for those figuring out God, Google, and grace."
—*Renee Johnson*, Devotional Diva™ spirited speaker and writer to the 20somethings

"It's a perfect resource for small groups or Sunday School classes. Through this book, you'll not only see Jesus formed more deeply in you, you might even discover Him smiling back at you in your text messages and Facebook posts."
—*Bill Giovannetti*, pastor, author of How to Keep Your Inner Mess from Trashing Your Outer World, and professor at A. W. Tozer Theological Seminary

iF@ith

Connecting with God
in the 21st Century

Daniel Darling

New Hope
PUBLISHERS

Birmingham, Alabama

New Hope® Publishers
P. O. Box 12065
Birmingham, AL 35202-2065
www.newhopepublishers.com
New Hope Publishers is a division of WMU®.

© 2011 by Dan Darling
All rights reserved. First printing 2011.
Printed in the United States of America.

No part of this publication may be reproduced, stored in a retrieval system, or transmitted in any form or by any means—electronic, mechanical, photocopying, recording, or otherwise—without the prior written permission of the publisher.

Library of Congress Cataloging-in-Publication Data
Darling, Daniel, 1978-
  iFaith : connecting with God in the 21st century / Daniel Darling.
    p. cm.
  ISBN 978-1-59669-294-7 (sc)
  1. Spiritual life--Christianity. 2. Spiritual life--Biblical teaching. I. Title.
  BV4501.3.D3735 2011
  248.4--dc22
                         2010026741

Scripture quotations marked ESV are from *The Holy Bible,* English Standard Version, copyright © 2001 by Crossway Bibles, a division of Good News Publishers. Used by permission. All rights reserved.

Scripture quotations marked NLT are taken from the *Holy Bible,* New Living Translation, copyright © 1996. Used by permission of Tyndale House Publishers, Inc., Wheaton, Illinois. All rights reserved.

Scripture quotations marked KJV are taken from *The Holy Bible*, King James Version.

ISBN-10: 1-59669-294-4
ISBN-13: 978-1-59669-294-7

N114131• 0111 • 4M1

More New Hope books by Dan Darling

Teen People of the Bible:
Celebrity Profiles of Real Faith and Tragic Failure

Crash Course:
Forming a Faith Foundation for Life

Dedication

To Pastor Bill Swanger, colaborer in the ministry

You have been a sovereign grace gift from God.
Thanks for taking the time to invest in me,
as mentor and friend.
The next breakfast is on me.

Table of Contents

INTRODUCTION 13

CHAPTER ONE
Read Receipt: A History of Waiting 19

CHAPTER TWO
Urgent Email: The Prayer of the Desperate 31

CHAPTER THREE
Prayer in ALL CAPS: Venting at God 43

CHAPTER FOUR
Blue-Screen Faith: The Impossible Prayer 59

CHAPTER FIVE
Reboot Your Life:
The Message in the Meltdown 75

CHAPTER SIX

The World's First Prayer Meeting:

Prayer and Faith in an Age of Progress   89

CHAPTER SEVEN

When God Is Offline:

How to Pray When the Lights Go Out   105

CHAPTER EIGHT

Your Divine Hotspot:

Staying Connected in a Disconnected World 117

CHAPTER NINE

Trojan Horse: The Virus That Disconnects   137

CHAPTER TEN

Friend Me:

Face-to-Face Friendship in a Digital World   153

RESOURCES   158

Acknowledgments

I'm deeply grateful for the many people who made this book happen:

Once again, Andrea Mullins, for believing and investing in me. You've become more than a publisher. You're a great friend.

The rest of the staff at New Hope: Joyce Dinkins, editor extraordinaire; Jonathan Howe, who has a brilliant grasp on the publishing industry; Ashley Stephens, who tirelessly answers all my emails and requests.

I'm deeply grateful to Cecil Murphey for telling me this book had potential and for his willingness to invest in my writing career. That writing clinic was a transformative experience.

My good friend, Pastor Dave Ralph, who read every chapter. Dave is one of the smartest and most winsome guys I know. Not only does he know theology, but he is also good at English. He provided critical feedback.

I'm deeply grateful for my church, Gages Lake Bible Church, for allowing me to write and encouraging God's work in me. I'm privileged to serve you as pastor. I love you guys like family.

Lastly, I want to thank my dear wife. This book was written during one of the most intense periods of our marriage, during and after the birth of our daughter, Emma, and during some intense health issues with our children. Angela endured my many late nights of writing. She is a patient, wonderful, godly wife. I'm blessed to be her husband.

introduction

A Connected Generation

In the waning months of 2008, as a historic new president carefully planned his transition team, he faced an agonizing choice that his 43 predecessors never faced in their 200-plus years of leading the United States. What was the question at hand?

Troop levels in Iraq?

The imploding financial sector?

The right pick for Education Secretary?

No, President Obama wrestled with this question: *Do I give up my BlackBerry?*

To George Washington, Abraham Lincoln, and even Ronald Reagan a blackberry was a semisweet, low-hanging fruit. But to President Obama it was a lifeline.

Obama became the first President from the "connected generation," accustomed to life attached to a small device that allows a person to make phone calls, send email, and text people around the globe. Security concerns, privacy acts, and records requirements were the main reasons experts counseled him to throw the BlackBerry in the Potomac.

But the Commander in Chief got his wish—his highly secure, encrypted, military-issued BlackBerry. He famously said, "They will pry my BlackBerry from my cold, dead hands."

Now, I thought that was a little extreme. I'm an iPhone guy.

Raised on Instant

The President's predicament is our predicament. We're members of the always-connected generation, weaned on warped speed, raised on instant. Instant formula. Disposable diapers. Satellite TV. GPS navigation. Online check-in.

In my three decades or so on this earth, life has moved from high-speed to warp speed. We email, IM, Facebook and Twitter. We text, YouTube, MMS, and Skype. Our ever-expanding, never-enough, always-on collection of devices explodes with data traveling at the speed of thought.

When we have a question, we send a digital message. When we want an answer, we demand a real-time reply.

In every area of life, from food to fashion to family life, we want bigger bandwidth, better pictures, faster delivery. We opt for the drive-through, express lane, and self-checkout.

If something is not immediately available at our fingertips, we don't worry. Because in a month Google or Apple will have an app for it.

God, Google, and Grace

Warning: this isn't a book that trashes technology and longs for the false idealism of a bygone era when everyone went to diners with 50 cent hamburgers, husbands and wives never argued, the music was always pure, and everyone lived blissfully like the Cleaver family.

We live here, in the twenty-first century. I believe God has a mission for *this* millennium. Plus, the good old days of the 1950s probably weren't as Norman Rockwell as we'd like to think.

However, as a card-carrying member of the "instant generation," I think we need to ask ourselves, *What effect has our hustling and bustling, hurrying and worrying had on our communication with God?*

In some ways, we really get it. We get—and like—receiving information and communication. And answers. One-on-one.

Before the modern age, the primary method of communication was the letter. Even well into the twentieth century, letter-writing was common, as telegraphs and telephones were used only in an emergency.

Letters were often heartfelt, poignant, and detailed. Writers maximized their limited opportunities to communicate. They approached a letter as if painting a masterpiece, carefully weighing the significance of each word and phrase.

The late nineteenth and early twentieth centuries ushered in the march of progress and the rapid acceleration of communication. As telephone usage increased, letter-writing declined and with it, the careful choice of words.

Fast-forward to the end of the twentieth century and the rapid growth of the Internet. The lost art of letter-writing was revived, but this time in digital form. Communication across towns, states, and continents became as easy as the click of a button. We might actually argue that people communicate *more* than they did in previous generations.

Twenty years ago, you would never call a friend in South Africa, unless you had a second job to pay the long-distance fees. Now you can use Skype, and not only talk, but actually see the person's face (which is good or bad, depending on whether or not you're eating breakfast at the time of the call).

Today, communication leaps across borders, time zones, and oceans. Seemingly, nobody is ever out of reach, unavailable, or offline.

And yet our sense of immediacy can be a handicap. I know, because I see it in myself. Studying for several sermons a week, handling the minutiae of small church life, writing books and articles, and raising a young family often leave me pressed for time. So when the lunch hour arrives, I usually hustle down the hallway to the kitchen, grab a frozen entrée, and aim for a ten-minute lunch.

I find the microwave and plop the instant meal on the turntable.

I punch two minutes on the keypad and bingo. The light comes on and the machine roars to life.

Then I wait.

And wait some more.

Those two minutes seem like two hours. Never mind that generations before had to forage into the wilderness, find an animal, shoot it, dress it, cook it, and eat it.

I'm impatient because I can't wait two minutes for an instant meal.

My irritation with the microwave is a symptom of our generation. We are not only be impatient. We are demanding, restive. Impatient with appliances. Demanding with people. Even restive with God.

Our prayer lives function like cosmic email. We fire off message after message and wait uneasily for the "ding" that brings the satisfaction of an instant answer.

Another Prayer Book?

Two things this book is not. It's not another how-to book on prayer by a guy who spends five hours a day in deep meditation and has this whole "talking with God" thing figured out. That's admirable but that's not me. It's also not a book on how to find the illusive "balance" in life by growing a beard, joining a monastery, and renouncing all interaction with technology.

This book is a journey with some of the real people in the Bible who didn't Twitter, text, or tote a BlackBerry or iPad, but who learned how to communicate with God in a powerfully intimate way. Let's hope their lessons encourage us moderns to rekindle our love with the timeless spiritual disciplines.

read receipt
a history of waiting

O Lᴏʀᴅ, how long shall I cry for help, and you will not hear? Or cry to you "Violence!" and you will not save?
—Habakkuk 1:2 (ESV)

It occurs to me that I've never met anyone young and patient. We're all in a hurry. We don't like to miss one panel of a revolving door. Patience comes hard in a hurry-up society. Yet it's an essential quality, cultivated only in extended periods of waiting.
—Chuck Swindoll

Every few weeks an email pops into my inbox with a read receipt attached, a feature that automatically sends an email to the sender, letting them know that, *yes* I have dropped everything else in my life to read their all-important missive.

Read receipts bother me. Is it an unhealthy need for control? Maybe it's pride that says, "I may read your email. I may not read your email. And I really don't want you to know." So you know that I take delicious satisfaction when my email program gives me the option—send or don't send.

You can guess which I choose.

There is one kind of read receipt I'd love to send. Too bad it doesn't exist.

I'd like to send a read receipt to God. Wouldn't you? A little note that says, "Did You hear my prayer? And if so, would You click this box? Thank You, your humble servant, Dan."

Several years ago, my wife, Angela endured a confounding string of medical issues. For two years, her life was: visit a specialist, schedule a test, revisit the specialist, hear the shrugging nonanswer, try a new medicine, and experience no relief. That bad movie replayed over and over and over again as if on a cosmic loop.

The darkness of those years forced me to rethink my approach to prayer.

We know God hears us. We know God cares for our needs. We know we're important to God. After all, we learned this the first day of Sunday School.

But where is God when we need Him most? And why does He make us wait?

What I discovered during our roller coaster of uncertainty is that we were not the first Christians God made wait. In fact, waiting is a theme replayed in the lives of the great men and women who play a starring role on the big screen of Scripture.

Consider the family of Jewish patriarch, Abraham. He and his wife, Sarah, struggled to reconcile the reality of her infertility with God's lofty promise to plant in their home the seeds of a great nation. Abraham's own name, chosen by God, means, "father of a multitude." Imagine the mockery this brought among his peers, especially in a culture that placed a high value on fertility. A man's worth was weighed by the size of his family, and a woman's by her ability to bear children.

Yet every single year for 25 years, God's grand promise went unfulfilled. Twenty-five years of sleepless nights and tear-stained failure. Twenty-five years of answering the questions from friends and family with a shrug and forced smile.

These two faithful believers, who left everything in their hometown of Ur to follow the Lord, endured the searing pain of childlessness. The supposed "father of multitudes" was childless.

Finally, with Abraham at the ripe age of 100 and Sarah at 90, God answered. He touched Sarah's womb and delivered on His promise. Isaac was born.

Three generations later, Abraham's great-grandson Joseph saw his God-directed dream delayed. As a young man, Joseph experienced a powerful series of night visions. He discerned these dreams as a special call of God to leadership. This was exciting for Joseph, but to Joseph's father and brothers, they came off as fantasies of a spoiled family favorite.

Thirteen years would pass before Joseph would see the fulfillment of those dreams. In those 13 years, he was nearly killed by his brothers, sold as a slave into a foreign country, sent to prison on a false rape charge, and forgotten by a friend who had promised to negotiate a release. Finally, when it seemed Joseph would die alone, shamed, and forgotten, he got his break. At the age of 30, through circumstances only God could ordain, the once-favored son of Jacob ascended to that long-promised leadership role—he became prime minister of Egypt.

Those same royal courts crushed the aspirations of another Hebrew. As a prince in the house of Pharaoh, Moses' heart burned for the plight of his people, the Hebrews. As descendants of Joseph, the Hebrews had settled in the land of the Nile, and through several generations, built a nation within a nation. Their growing size and influence was seen as a threat to the new pharaoh's hold on the throne. He responded the only way power-threatened dictators know how to do: with severe oppression.

So Moses rejected the soft comfort of the palace and assumed the role of rescuer. He would lead his people against his own royal family. But when Moses put his plan into action, the Hebrews rejected his leadership. Moses was forced to flee Egypt, an embarrassed and shamed fugitive. He spent 40 years on the backside of nowhere, leading sheep until God finally fulfilled Moses' destiny and led him back to Egypt to lead Israel out of bondage.

God grew another Jewish leader from the obscure sheep fields. David was an unremarkable shepherd boy who nurtured a passion for God. But he was forgotten among Jesse's many sons. Then one day a man named Samuel, a prophet and priest in Israel, appeared at Jesse's house. He was under divine guidance to appoint the next king of Israel.

After combing through the impressive lineup of future leaders among Jesse's sons without receiving God's blessing, Samuel asked if there was anyone else. The father sheepishly mentioned his other son. The forgotten son. The "I-was-hoping-you-wouldn't-ask-me" son.

David was finally summoned to the presence of Samuel, who was directed by God to anoint David as the next king. Great, now what? Back to the humble sheep fields for David. No coronation ceremony. No crown. No throne.

At age 16, what David didn't know was that 14 long, hard years would pass before he would ever see that crown, that throne, that ceremony. And that was only the throne of Judah. Another 7½ years would pass before he assumed the throne over all of Israel.

Waiting is not a theology reserved only for the Old Testament. I'm intrigued by a subtle theme in Jesus' teaching on the Gospels. Often, when implored to demonstrate His deity, He would say, *"My hour has not yet come"* (John 2:4). Jesus resisted the urge of the immediate, submitting to the precise timing of the Father's will.

Paul, the world's first and greatest evangelist/church planter, endured his own long period of waiting. When we race through the books of Acts and Galatians, which chronicle Paul's journey from enemy of the Cross to defender of the faith, we often miss the silent years that transpired between his Damascus Road experience and the beginning of his itinerant ministry. Scripture is silent on Paul's thought process during that time, but I imagine a fiery former Pharisee burning with anticipation, longing for the day he could share the gospel with the world.

@

JESUS RESISTED THE URGE OF THE IMMEDIATE.

You must know that none of these believers waited with perfect trust in God's will. The Bible is not an anthology of specialized saints; it is the divine record of ordinary men and women whose faith was strengthened in the crucible of God's waiting room.

Like us, they grew impatient with God, tried to force God's hand, and often chafed against the slow pace of God's will.

Waiting: The DNA of Faith

Nearly 50 times the Scripture implores us to wait because waiting is the DNA of faith. The root Hebrew word might imply "waiting with eager expectation." In other words, *believing, against the odds, that God will be faithful to His promise.* This is a waiting that includes more than merely sitting idly by. It means holding on to your integrity, your values, your faith in God, even as circumstances seem to prove God wrong. It's an anticipation and longing that runs deep into the soul.

David breaks it down in Psalm 27:14, likely written during the future king's own angst-filled years spent running from the madman Saul. David spells out the two indispensable ingredients of a faith that waits— courage and strength.

Waiting reveals courage, the courage to hang on to your values when logic says to let go. But it builds strength.

Ask any successful athlete. He or she will tell you that strength doesn't come overnight (even in the age of steroids and human growth hormone). Strength is built over time, the accumulation of a daily, weekly, monthly, yearly regimen of disciplined training. Read the biographies of world-class performers. They'll share about early mornings in the gym, working, pushing, and sweating.

Our waiting years are God's gym, where He builds in us a stronger heart muscle. This is growth that can't be microwaved, truncated, or manufactured at warp speed. A durable faith is formed in the mundane disciplines of daily life, a straight line in the diligent pursuit of godliness (1 Timothy 4:8).

Lessons from God's Waiting Room

I think I've spent an entire lifetime in waiting rooms, either escorting my wife to her many specialists or awaiting the inevitable visits on behalf of my kids' various ailments. Each time I smart at the irony. We rush to get out the door, step on the pedal, and blast into the office, only to sit and wait. Thankfully all of our doctors carry up-to-date subscriptions of *Sports Illustrated* and *Newsweek*. And if not, well, there is my iPhone.

Still, the waiting room makes me restless as I mentally check off the work I'm not getting done. It's always an interesting ride home. Angela is routinely subjected to my verbal tirades against the medical establishments that seem to be at odds with my all-important schedule.

I've also spent significant time in God's waiting room, and while the reading material is fresher (the Bible, good Christian books), my restlessness is as acute. I remember my single years, how often I yearned for the love of a wife. I remember ticking off ministries I could have been doing if only God would hurry up His marital timeline. Little did I know that during those years, God was forming my character and also preparing a special woman, Angela, who arrived from Texas, via Germany, to Chicago to be my wife. (It's a long story; stop by Chicago sometime, and I'll share the entire miracle.)

Maybe you're nervously fidgeting today in God's waiting room. It could be the pursuit of answers to a medical crisis. It could be the impossibility of finding a job in a tough market. It could be the hope of finding true love. Everyone's waiting room looks different, and yet, God's purpose is always the same.

I've always found comfort in the words of the obscure Old Testament prophet Habakkuk. His anguished cry, "How long?" echoes the pleas from our own impatient hearts.

Here Habakkuk sat as God's chosen prophet, wondering when God would follow through on His promise to punish evil and reward good in Judah. His impatient words read like a challenge to the Almighty, as if His credibility was at stake.

God's answers are like medicine to a heart that yearns for hope:

- *When God is silent, God is active.* God told Habakkuk, *"Look around at the nations; look and be amazed! For I am doing something in your own day, something you wouldn't believe even if someone told you about it"* (Habakkuk 1:5 NLT). At the very moment of Habakkuk's desperate prayer, God was raising up the Babylonian army as the solution to Israel's disobedience. And when we're in the waiting room, when it seems all of God's activity has ground to a halt, God is behind the curtain, moving the characters and pieces in place on the stage of our lives.

- *God's solution often comes from an unexpected source.* God's chosen method of punishing Israel was unexpected. The Babylonians were more depraved than Israel and yet they were God's solution to Israel's disobedience. In Habakkuk's world, Babylon was in no position to be a sovereign ally. They would get judged by God, but not before they were used as an effective chastisement against God's own people. The lesson for us in God's answer to Habakkuk is that God often brings resolution to our situation from an unlikely source. He's not limited by our carefully crafted scenarios.

- *God's timing is always perfect.* God said to Habakkuk and says to us: "*My will is executed with precise timing. I'm not early. I'm not late*" (Habakkuk 2:3 ESV). God is not hurried by our manufactured sense of urgency. He's not impressed by our demands for answers. He operates according to a divine clock that isn't moved up by our twenty-first-century sense of rush.

- *God is worthy of worship, regardless of our circumstances.* I love Habakkuk's response to God. Chapter 3 could be read at every Thanksgiving celebration. The humbled prophet says, "*Though the fig tree should not blossom, nor fruit be on the vines, the produce of the olive fail and the fields yield no food, the flock be cut off from the fold and there be no herd in the stalls, yet I will rejoice in the Lord; I will take joy in the God of my salvation. God, the Lord, is my strength; he makes my feet like the deer's; he makes me tread on my high places.*

To the choirmaster: with stringed instruments"
(Habakkuk 3:17–19 ESV). Here's the question we must ask: Will we worship God in the waiting rooms of life? Or will we only worship Him on the mountaintops? Can the Christian employee praise God when he is given a pink slip? Can the single person praise God when there are no prospects for marriage? Can the childless couple praise God when they fail to conceive? Can the pastor praise God even as he sees declining attendance?

Waiting is considered loathsome to a generation accustomed to having quick answers, fast results, and instant gratification. But we must surrender our hearts to the sovereignty of God who slows us down, because waiting is not wasted time at all. Waiting is the essence of a faith that pleases Him.

Questions

- If God intervened tomorrow and changed your situation, would that enable you to trust Him more fully? Would it make Him a better God?
- In what way do you attempt to advance the timing of God's agenda?
- Has this strategy helped? Has it hindered?

Resources

I've always enjoyed studying the characters of the Bible. Two resources, one new and one old, really make these people come alive:

- The "Great Lives" series by Chuck Swindoll. I'll never forget my first introduction to Dr. Swindoll's biographical teaching series. I was in the car on the way to work after classes and his series on Moses was featured on the radio. I actually was late for work several days.
- *Bible Characters* by Alexander Whyte. This is a terrific series by a preacher of several generations ago.

Bible

- Abraham—Genesis 11–21
- Joseph—Genesis 30–47
- Moses—Exodus 2; Acts 7; Hebrews 13
- David—1 and 2 Samuel
- Paul—Galatians 2:1–10; Acts 9–28
- Habakkuk—Habakkuk 1–3

urgent email
the prayer of the desperate

She said to them, "Do not call me Naomi; call me Mara, for the Almighty has dealt very bitterly with me. I went away full, and the Lord has brought me back empty. Why call me Naomi, when the Lord has testified against me and the Almighty has brought calamity upon me?"
—Ruth 1:20–21 (ESV)

We assume life is supposed to work in ways that make us feel the way we want to feel, the way we intuitively and irresistibly sense we are designed to feel. We further assume that if there is a God, His job is to do what we cannot do to make life work as we want. The good news of the gospel is not that God will provide a way to make life easier. The good news of the gospel, for this life, is that He will make our lives better.
—Larry Crabb

There are emails. There are important emails. And there are urgent emails. Ever get one of those?

If an email is flagged with a red exclamation point, you know you'd better act fast.

You hang up the phone.

You put down the coffee.

You begin typing.

Not simultaneously, of course.

Urgency visits me more frequently in my new role as a pastor. Urgency waits impatiently on the church stoop as I arrive on Tuesday morning. Urgency knocks loudly on my door. I'm discovering that pastors sit uniquely at the nexus of human need and spiritual application.

When I receive an urgent message, whether email or text or IM or voice mail, a rotten feeling hits my gut.

It's the "uh-oh-something's-wrong" feeling.

When Ashli's phone number appeared on Angela's caller ID, we both got that feeling. Angela dug deep inside her purse and hit the green button on her cell. I watched as she listened to her best friend, whose anguished cries echoed through the phone. Tears streamed down Angela's face as she responded in the most human and yet biblical way.

"Weep with those who weep" (Romans 12:15 ESV).

Ashli wept. Angela wept. I wept.

Ashli's husband, Ben, a robust man of 30, recently reunited with the church, faithful father, beloved boss and co-worker, was diagnosed with a fatal form of cancer.

The news hit us hard. It wasn't that long ago that Angela and I flew to Las Vegas to be part of Ashli and Ben's wedding. It was a joyous occasion as we watched two of our favorite people in the world begin their journey together. They had great plans to build a life together.

The dreadful news of Ben's diagnosis came just as they were getting started on that life. Six years of marriage had yielded two beautiful children, a growing career for Ben, and a new series of ministries at their local church.

Now, everything Ashli longed for was being snatched away. For the next 12 months, Ashli's prayers reflected the desperate strains of an aching heart. They were like urgent emails to the heavenly Father.

Little Miss Sunshine No More

Centuries earlier, tragedy arrived at the doorstep of another good woman. Naomi, whose name means "lovely" or "pleasant," was a devout Jewish girl who married her sweetheart, a God-fearing man whose name means "God is my king."

Naomi seemed destined for the good life. That's what is supposed to happen when "Lovely" marries "God Is My King." But reality has a nasty way of smudging the tranquility of our Thomas Kinkade life, doesn't it? In a female replay of Job, Naomi's life produced a series of heartbreaking misfortunes.

Their hometown of Bethlehem, a city known as the "house of bread," was sweating out a country-wide famine. It was the direct result of God's judgment for Israel's brazen sin, a fate warned by God through the prophets, but unheeded by the nation. Naomi lived in a shameful time in Israel's history, an era of lawlessness, anarchy, and sexual license. Several times, the Book of Judges describes this era as one in which *everyone did what was right in his own eyes* (Judges 17:6; 21:25 ESV). But Naomi and Elimelech were different, faithful in a culture of unfaithfulness. Yet their faith didn't spare them the effects of God's judgment on His people.

Famine is a word Americans barely understand. Even in a time of recession, few know what it feels like to go to bed hungry.

I'll never forget the image of little children picking at a garbage pile while I was on a missions trip to India. I saw the same images in travels to Cairo, Gaza, and parts of Mexico. The haunting images of extreme poverty have never left my consciousness.

Today, many around the world live in poverty. According to the site, stopthehunger.org, more than 17,000 people die *every single day* from starvation.

So you can understand why Elimelech, "God is my king," elected to move his family to Moab. No doubt this faithful Jewish family cringed at the thought of leaving the land of their fathers to live where the people worshipped the pagan god Chemosh, a false deity whose worship demanded child sacrifice.

Birthed from the incestuous relationship between Lot and his daughter, Moab is referred to in Scripture as *"God's washpot"* (Psalm 108:9 KJV). The Moabites were forbidden to enter the assembly of the Jewish people until the tenth generation.

Many Bible commentators offer harsh condemnation of this family's move to Moab, but Elimelech and Naomi were desperate. And we know their move was intended as a temporary trip. Their hearts were still in the land Yahweh promised.

So here is Naomi, forced out of her homeland, separated from her people and familiar culture, walking the long, dusty road to a the last place on earth they wanted to call home. Moving to another country, another culture, is difficult in any time. But imagine the hostility in Moab. No Statue of Liberty beckoned "the tired, the poor, the huddled masses yearning to breathe free." I'm sure discrimination against the Hebrews was severe. I'm sure the family worried about Elimelech beginning a new career. What would he do? How would they support themselves? But that was the just the beginning.

Not long after the boxes were unpacked and the miniblinds were installed, Elimelech suddenly died. Now Naomi faced life in this foreign wasteland as a single mother. Any hopes of returning to Israel were surely dashed.

And life would not get easier. Naomi's two sons married Moabite woman, but neither bore children. For ten long years the family suffered the sting of the barren womb, a bitter curse in a day when fertility was seen as a sign of supernatural blessing.

Then the unthinkable happened. Naomi's two sons died. We often read this part of her bio as a footnote to the larger drama of the Book of Ruth, but we should linger here. As a young father, I recoil at the very thought of burying any of my No ORGANIZED CHURCH. three children. Nobody writes that as a part of their family's future. And yet for Naomi, it was reality.

Now Naomi was completely helpless—a destitute widow in a foreign land. In those days, widows had no support system. No Social Security. No charitable organizations. No organized church.

Carolyn Custis James, in her remarkable book *The Gospel of Ruth,* describes the harshness of Naomi's situation. "Overnight, her already diminished social status hit rock bottom, and Naomi was suddenly at risk. Without a male connection, she had no place in society and no source of income. Without a male protector, she was fair game for the unscrupulous who regularly preyed on helpless widows. Alone in a male-dominated world, Naomi was cast upon the mercy of a society that had no interest in her."

You might not blame Naomi for wondering what God was up to. There she was, a faithful follower of the true God in an unfaithful time. And yet her faith was rewarded by an unbelievable series of tragedies.

Naomi's life forces us to question our Westernized version of Christianity, that often sends the message that a life of faith is always followed by prosperity and is devoid of problems.

As I've studied the life of Naomi, I've been shocked by the near-universal condemnation of Naomi's attitude by commentators, preachers, and authors. Most point to her first words as she crawled back in humility to her hometown. She told people, "Please don't call me lovely and pleasant, call me Mara. *Mara* means, 'bitter.'" So most offer the knee-jerk reaction, "Naomi is bitter. She's angry. She needs to get over it."

Funny, but they sound strangely familiar to Job's three discouraging friends. How easy it is to dispense bullet-point theology when it is not our lives in the crucible.

What we miss about Naomi is her authentically raw expression of faith in the Lord. Stop and consider *all* of her words: *"Do not call me Naomi; call me Mara, for the Almighty has dealt very bitterly with me. I went away full, and the LORD has brought me back empty. Why call me Naomi, when the LORD has testified against*

me and the Almighty has brought calamity upon me?"
(Ruth 1:20–21 ESV).

Did you catch that? She may not have liked what
she got from God. *But she acknowledged that it came
from Him.* Naomi wasn't performing cartwheels of joy,
but she didn't abandon God either. Weaved between the
tears is a powerful expression of God's sovereignty in
the brokenness of her life.

A Less Tidy Faith

Naomi's story echoes our own. Somewhere along the
line, a famous preacher or best-selling author told us
that if we "just trust in Jesus," or if we "just give enough
money," or if we "just attend church faithfully," or if we
"just follow the rules," then life will automatically get so
much better. There are even whole books and sermons
available that teach "the right kind of prayer" that trig-
gers the blessings from heaven.

But what happens when you follow Christ in faith
and life gets worse?

What happens when a devoted young woman
pursues the call of ministry, attends Bible college,
marries a would-be preacher, only to see him walk off
with the secretary?

What happens when parents endeavor to raise their
children in the Lord, following biblical principles, only
to see those kids wander from the faith?

What happens when your spiritual role models fall
into serious sin or use their position to abuse and hurt
those they are called to serve?

What happens when life takes an unexpected turn?
It rips the false sheen off our hollow theology. We're

forced to come to grips with the naked reality that following God is often a life filled with hardship and cross-bearing.

You can accurately line up Naomi's suffering with Job's, with one interesting difference. Naomi's life doesn't have quite the tidy ending of Job's. Everything Job lost, he got back, and it was doubled: bigger house, more sons, bigger barns, more property.

Naomi didn't get that payoff. But you'll find that her reward was far richer than any material gains. She rebounded from her devastating losses by investing in her daughter-in-law, Ruth.

Naomi had no reason to see Ruth succeed. Ruth was a Moabite woman. She was from another generation. She was a constant reminder of the loss of her sons.

Yet God worked through Naomi's brokenness not only to impact the life of a new believer in the living Lord, but also to impact God's people, Israel, and to fulfill the outworking of His ultimate plan of redemption. It's quite an epic story.

Ruth married Boaz. One of their great-grandchildren was David, the shepherd boy plucked from obscurity and anointed king over Israel. From this family would come Jesus, the promised Messiah.

As I write this, I think of our friend Ashli. She's nearly three years removed from that fateful phone call. Like Naomi, her life hasn't had the tidy ending. For an entire year, she lived through the roller coaster of a spouse with cancer. At times we thought God was answering our prayers and healing Ben. Other times it seemed God was astonishingly silent. During Thanksgiving of 2008 we traveled from Chicago and spent a few days with Ashli and Ben, celebrating a milestone in his recovery.

But the celebration was short-lived. A few months later, Ben's body couldn't fight any longer and he slipped into the arms of Jesus.

Now Ashli is left raising two children on her own. We don't know why God took Ben, just like Naomi never fully understood why God took her husband and two sons. But Ashli can hang on to the truth that God will be glorified and will bring about good from this unspeakable tragedy.

Conditioned for the Good Life

Naomi's story, Ashli's story—these narratives frighten my generation, because we're conditioned for the good life. We've been fed a steady diet of positive empowerment. We've grown spiritually fat on the junk food of bad theology and political promises of prosperity.

There is nothing inherently wrong with prosperity or the good life. But is the American dream the sum total of our spiritual aspirations? If so, we've missed something. What Christ offers is something radically different. Take up your cross, He says. Follow Me, He asks. Deny yourself, He commands.

Cross-bearing? Following? Denying? These words are insulting to a generation conditioned for unlimited success. Sure, we'll follow Christ, but there better be a safety net. At least a 401(k) and health insurance.

The Prayers of the Desperate

I believe Naomi's life represents the journey God desires for every one of His followers. When life moves from pleasant to bitter, it is not God that must change. It is not our circumstances that must change. It is our theology that must change.

Rather than assuming God owes us the good life, or wondering why life has been so unfair, we must square with the truth of God's revelation in the Scriptures. It is this: to follow God is to follow His Son, Jesus Christ. And to follow Christ is to accept the way of the Cross, the path of suffering. Not because God is intent on our displeasure, but because God is intent on our holiness.

From Naomi's life we learn three powerful lessons:

Your struggles may point others to God. Naomi's gritty demonstration of faith had a transformative effect on her daughter-in-law, Ruth. Ruth observed Naomi up close during all those years of tragedy, from the death of her husband, to the agonizing over the childlessness of her sons' families, to the death of her sons. None wrested Naomi's grip on Jehovah. Her faith, in a swirling cacophony of trial, seemed illogical at times. It went against the grain of the culture. You can hear the whispers, *What is your Jehovah doing for you now?* And yet it was Naomi's unrelenting faith in the midst of her darkest hours that led Ruth to say, *"Your people shall be my people, and your God my God"* (Ruth 1:16 ESV).

We rarely consider that our trials, the unfair tragedies that roll across the threshold of good people, may be the very signposts that lead others to God.

Our problems are always vertical and not horizontal. Hidden in Naomi's seemingly bitter rant in Ruth 1:20 is her trust in the sovereignty of God. Her laundry list of Job-like sufferings gave her several options. She could have denied the existence of God altogether and pursued the more culturally convenient worship of the Moab god Chermish. She could have lashed out at the people in her life or the poor environment that led to the death of her husband and sons. Instead, Naomi accepted her fate as the divine will of God.

The denial of God—the blind faith in human reasoning—is little salve to the wounds of tragedy. But to believe God permitted the sufferings as part of His larger purpose on earth at least brings the assurance that Someone is in control and that in the end, all things will work together for our good (Romans 8:28). There can be no hope without a giver of hope. There can be no assurance without Someone to assure it. There can be no peace without a Prince of Peace.

Suffering is the syllabus for ministry. Naomi's trust in God allowed her to use redemptively her sufferings for God's glory in the life of Ruth. They became the building blocks of a mentoring ministry whose fruits reached beyond her little world.

We must be careful not to waste our tragedies. Once we've picked up the pieces of our faith, we have a treasure to be poured into the lives of those God has uniquely thrust into our world. Today I consider myself a rich man for the wise older pastors who use the grit of their years in ministry to enrich my life.

To a generation who longs for the good life, suffering seems a cruel twist of fate by a God who seems detached, distant, or even devious. But we have hope that the cross we carry doesn't surprise the heavenly Father, but is deliberately designed for our holiness.

Questions

- How can God use your present struggle to make a difference in others? in the world?
- What about Naomi's story scares you?
- What wrong attitudes about God lead you to think you deserve a life free from suffering?

Resources

- Two years ago I was driving in my car (why is it that my best inspiration happens in a 1996 Nissan Sentra?) when I heard a conversation on WMBI's (90.1 Chicago) Midday Connection program on the subject of Ruth. The hosts were chatting with author Carolyn Custis James. They were discussing her book, *The Gospel of Ruth*. I soon bought the book and discovered an entirely new way of looking at Naomi, who has always been seen by commentators as a bitter old woman. James' in-depth research and biblical accuracy formed the basis of my new and profound respect for this "female Job" of the Old Testament. Needless to say, I highly recommend this book.

Bible

- Ruth 1–4
- James 1
- Matthew 16:24
- Mark 8:34
- Luke 9:23
- Romans 8:28

prayer in ALL CAPS
Venting at God

My feet had almost stumbled,
my steps had nearly slipped.
For I was envious of the arrogant
when I saw the prosperity of the wicked.
—Psalm 73:2 (ESV)

The Psalms record deep devotion, intense feeling, exalted
emotion, and dark dejection. They play upon the keyboard of
the human soul with all the stops pulled out.
—J. Vernon McGee

Somewhere, sometime; the people in charge of the digital superhighway anointed the CAPS key the ultimate expression of anger. (I'm envisioning ten guys with dark glasses in a smoke-filled room at Google's headquarters.)

For many years I fielded the Web response at a large media ministry. Each week brought dozens of hastily written, poorly spelled missives, most of which began with the dire warning that our organization was on the verge of experiencing the hot wrath of God because of a doctrinal difference.

ALL CAPS is the official venting button of the BlackBerry generation. From urgent Facebook entries to angry anonymous political comments on news sites and blogs, we're a people who easily ditch social norms to express outright anger.

Screaming at God

Most of us would like to think these digital scream- ers are extreme members of pajama-wearing minor- ity with plenty of idle time to spend at the computer in their parents' basement. We'd like to think the rest of us dignified working folks have neither the time nor the absence of dignity to lower ourselves in this way. But we'd have to confess that if given just the right mix of circumstance and opportunity, we too are capable of letting such angry words fly.

Especially when it comes to our conversations with God, I think there is a little screamer in all of us, wish- ing we could pull out the divine keyboard and fire off an ALL CAPS email at the heavenly Father.

WHY DID YOU LET ME LOSE MY JOB?
WHY DID YOU LET MY SPOUSE LEAVE ME?
WHY DID I GET CANCER?
WHY CAN'T WE HAVE CHILDREN?
WHY DID MY SON DIE ON THE BATTLEFIELD?

I know what you're thinking. *I wouldn't dare talk like that to God.* But have you noticed that some of the most revered men and women in the Bible did? They may not have had an ALL CAPS key, but they were unafraid to verbalize their honest, outright frustrations with the Almighty.

A History of Biblical Screaming

You might be surprised at who had the guts to speak like this to God.

Abraham and Sarah laughed hard at God's promise to give them a child (Genesis 17:17; 18:2). It wasn't a laugh of mirth; but one of bitter sarcasm at the sheer impossibility of Sarah bearing a child in her old age.

Moses, known as the meekest man in the Bible, lashed out in frustration at the intractable people God called him to lead. The New Living Translation shares Moses' gripe:

> *And Moses said to the LORD, "Why are you treating me, your servant, so harshly? Have mercy on me! What did I do to deserve the burden of all these people? Did I give birth to them? Did I bring them into the world? Why did you tell me to carry them in my arms like a mother carries a nursing baby? How can I carry them to the land you swore to give their ancestors? Where am I supposed to get meat for all these people? They keep whining to me, saying, 'Give us meat to eat! I can't carry all these people by myself! The load is far too heavy! If this is how you intend to treat me, just go ahead and kill me. Do me a favor and spare me this misery!"* (Numbers 11:11–15 NLT).

That's not a prayer you'll see printed in fancy script on a greeting card.

There are the prophets, whose rants at the Almighty fill pages of the Old Testament. One, Jeremiah, wrote an entire book filled with them. It's called Lamentations.

But maybe the greatest anthology of human venting is found in the Psalms. Collected throughout Jewish history, psalms were the music of the Hebrew soul—part prayer, part melody.

I find it interesting when we open our Bibles to the very center, we don't discover doctrine or narrative or history. Instead, we're plunged deep into the heart of man's relationship with God as revealed in the Psalms.

Of course, we know the divisions of Scripture are man-made, so it would be ridiculous to divine a life-changing principle from the placement of a particular book. Still, I don't think it's a coincidence that God allowed the Bible to be published in such a way that the Psalms were placed in the center. One thing we can be sure of is that the Holy Spirit, in His divine inspiration of the Scriptures, chose as part of the canon the tender words of broken men spoken to the Almighty.

Dr. Warren Wiersbe speaks of the Psalms value: "The book of Psalms has been and still is the irreplaceable devotional guide, prayer book, and hymnal of the people of God." Reformer John Calvin agrees: "They are the anatomy of all parts of the soul."

The Psalms are a rich variety of songs, poems, and prayers. Some are prophetic, some offer thanksgiving, some share Israel's history. But 50 stand alone as psalms of *lament*. Some well-known laments are Psalm 2 that asks, *"Why do the heathen rage?"* and Psalm 22 with its Messianic foreshadowing, *"My God, My God, why hast thou forsaken me?"* (KJV). Yet, I'm not sure any lament touches everyday life quite like Psalm 73.

Psalm 73 was not written by David or Moses, but by a lesser-known man named Asaph, a respected musician appointed by David to the distinguished position as director of the King's Choir (1 Chronicles 16:5). Asaph's work was celebrated by generations of Jewish people (2 Chronicles 29:30; Nehemiah 12:46). At least 12 Psalms bear his signature.

So when you read Asaph's words in Psalm 73, you know they are not the words of a bitter, spiritually disconnected soul. They are the honest questions shared in anguish by a man walking intimately with his God.

Upside-Down Truth

I can't claim the spiritual credentials of Asaph, but having grown up in the evangelical world, I've known prayer to be a part of my life since birth.

I remember kneeling every night at the foot of my parents' bed as the family gathered to pray. I remember refreshing Wednesday night prayer meetings, where we heard people ask prayer for everything from ailing oak trees to the conversion of distant cousins. And we always prayed before our meals as if to not pray was to invite the terror of God (or at the very least, the poisoning of the casserole.)

But somewhere along the way, I seemed to have developed a habit of lifeless, robotic, "safe" prayers, which are theologically beautiful, but coldly impersonal.

So when I first read Asaph's prayer, it took me back. How can Asaph be so angry, so honest, so raw and get away with it? You'll notice that though Asaph is angry, he doesn't approach God as an enemy. He approaches Him as a believer of God's promise to be good to those who are pure of heart. He actually repeated God's conditional covenant: if Israel earnestly followed the Lord, they would experience His rich blessings (Leviticus 26; Deuteronomy 28–30).

In fact, it was this very promise of God that was the problem for Asaph. It appeared that Yahweh was not holding up His end of the bargain.

The Missing Shalom

The first time I read Psalm 73, I assumed Asaph was wrestling with some garden-variety envy, the typical American lusting after a neighbor's bigger boat or house or 401(k) plan. Maybe he hated that his neighbor got three weeks at his vacation house in West Palm Beach or he wished his kids could go to prep school like their rich cousins.

Asaph is struggling with something more. He's experiencing a crisis of faith. Listen carefully:

But as for me, my feet had almost stumbled, my steps had nearly slipped (Psalm 73:2 ESV).

Asaph says his feet nearly slipped. Asaph wasn't simply discouraged or exhausted. He was on the verge of a complete physical and emotional breakdown. Worse, he was in danger of losing his faith.

Nineteenth-century author Charles Spurgeon writes: "Asaph could make no progress in the good road; his feet ran away from under him like those of a man on a sheet of ice. He was weakened for all practical action, and in great danger of actual sin, and so of a disgraceful fall."

A spiritual leader was about to fall from grace.

Nobody wants to think someone like Asaph could experience an "epic fall." Good Christians aren't supposed to wrestle with doubt. But they often do. Consider the sad case of Dr. Charles Templeton. Dr. Templeton was a pioneer in Youth for Christ International, the youth organization that birthed the extended ministry of Billy Graham. He and Graham preached to packed stadiums across the world in the 1950s and 1960s, sharing the gospel of Jesus Christ. But in the late 1950s, Dr. Templeton shocked the evangelical world by renouncing his faith. His story is told by Lee Strobel in Strobel's best-selling book, *The Case for Christ.*

Asaph didn't go as far as Templeton. The word *almost* tells us Asaph's journey didn't lead him off the spiritual cliff, but perilously close. But why?

For Asaph, it wasn't the wicked in other nations that troubled him. He trusted God's providence to take care of them in His time. It was the wicked in his own country, among God's people, the religious frauds who professed God's truth in the Temple, but denied it throughout the week. Bible teacher, Bob Deffinbaugh explains:

> *Asaph's vantage point was from the perspective of the choir loft. I can almost see him there in the temple, looking out over the congregation. They had healthy, well-fed bodies, fine clothes, and expensive jewelry. He had aches and pains, meager clothing, and no luxuries of life. He was serving God; they were not. It wasn't fair.*

Nothing shatters a person's faith like spiritual hypocrisy, when people you love and admire talk one way and walk another.

You know who I'm talking about. You see them on Sunday. They come all dressed up, and they play the part to perfection. They smile broadly on Sunday, open the doors for the women, and throw large sums of money in the offering plate. They meet every spiritual checkmark (saying no to all the right things); they have the right Bible version; and they volunteer at every public event. Everyone insists on their deep spirituality. Yet Monday through Friday they treat their employees like slaves. They ignore their families. They worship at the altar of money and power. They bully and intimidate, leveraging Christianity to serve their own purposes and build their mini kingdoms.

To Asaph, God's promises were upside down. Psalm 73:3 shares his frustration at the "prosperity" of the wicked. The original Hebrew word for "prosperity" is *shalom*. If you've traveled to Israel or have spent time in the Jewish community, you'll know this is a familiar greeting of peace and goodwill. But in Asaph's time, *shalom* referred to the totality of the Lord's blessings, the physical and spiritual covenant between God and Israel. While some of God's *shalom* was unconditional (the sending of a Messiah, for instance), much of it was dependent on their obedience (Isaiah 32:17).

Asaph met the benchmark of obedience, and yet, God was pouring out His *shalom* on those who ignored Him. Asaph's doubt went to the very core of his faith. *Can God be trusted?*

Your Asaph Moments

Seasons of spiritual doubt are where the theological rubber hits the road, the place where faith becomes intensely personal. But the question is, what do we do with the questions?

Some lock them inside, projecting an image that everything is OK. Others unload their uncertainties on an army of friends. Others carry false guilt at the thought of questioning the Almighty.

Asaph employed all three and found no relief. Finally, he took his doubts about God's goodness to God Himself. That's right; Asaph entered the "sanctuary of God" not with a heart of praise or worship, but with a sack full of questions.

The newfound revelation for me, a lifelong, safe, churchgoing good boy, was that it is actually OK to question God. Asaph survived without lightning bolts from heaven, an opening of the earth to swallow him, or a sudden plague of leprosy.

Asaph's rants have caused me to question my own prayer life. Those nagging doubts, the raging questions, the unsettling questions that afflict our souls—why have I kept those from God? It seems to me that the very thing I wish to hide from Him is the very thing He wants to hear. We are encouraged to come "boldly" before the throne of God (Hebrews 4:16).

@

IT IS ACTUALLY OK TO QUESTION GOD.

As a matter of fact, if you study the life of every successful Bible character, you'll discover that each approached God this way.

That's why Peter pleaded with Christians to cast their anxieties upon the Lord (1 Peter 5:7). I have to wonder if the fisherman-turned-apostle was envisioning of a kind of strategic casting.

Interestingly, this word used by Peter, *casting,* is translated from a Greek word *Epiripto* [ēp-pee-RIP-toh] used only one other time, in Luke 19:35, when the disciples *cast* their garments onto the colt Jesus was to ride into Jerusalem. It means to fling with intentionality. I'm thinking Peter is thinking back to this time on the high seas of Galilee, flinging those nets intentionally toward a new school of fish.

Peter seems to be saying to his readers: "Take that net of troubles, those problems you have with God, and throw them off your shoulders onto the ready mercy of your heavenly Father."

This kind of prayer really cuts to the heart of our view of God. We have to shed our wrong notions of Him as the pitiless schoolmarm, waiting for us to employ the perfect string of phrases before He lets loose of His grace. This is not the God of Asaph or Peter. This is not the God you serve.

The God of the Bible is a God ready for questions and doubts, for the pleadings of a heavy heart. He isn't surprised by our angry Asaph moments.

The Recombobulation Zone

I was unexpectedly reminded of this life-changing principle as I sat in the Milwaukee airport. I frequently fly out of Milwaukee's General Mitchell Airport because it's closer and easier than O'Hare.

I was thinking over Asaph's prayer in Psalm 73 when I looked up and saw a sign for a Recombobulation Zone. The sign points to a small space just past security.

The purpose is obvious. Passing through security usually leaves travelers a discombobulated mess of phones, carry-ons, keychains, shoes, and belts. So the hospitable people a General Mitchell Airport in Milwaukee provide soft music, cushioned chairs, and table space to help the harried traveler, like Humpty Dumpty, getting put back together again before boarding a flight.

I thought, *Wow, that's kind of like our time with God.* The sanctuary of God was Asaph's "recombobulation zone," where God glued the broken pieces of his life back together.

Every believer must periodically enter this zone. Instead of soft music, cushioned chairs, and table space, God provides comfort, wisdom, and hope through meditation on His Word and prayer. Quiet time with the Father is the Sabbath rest our restless souls need and crave.

Your sanctuary may be early in the morning, it may be late at night, it may be in the car or in the shower. Where and when and how you meet God doesn't matter. What matters is that you make time to go there and spend time in the recombulation zone of God's love. A fragile faith needs *repeated* visits, unplugged from the rest of the world.

Asaph's time with God reshaped his theology with five fresh truths from the heart of God:

- **He's God and we're not.** Our default position is to look at life horizontally, through the dirty prism of injustice. Yet, *"brutish and foolish"* is how Asaph described this outlook (Psalm 73:17–18). Is he belittling his struggle? No. He is simply acknowledging his lack of understanding compared to the wisdom of God. Consider what the Lord told the prophet Isaiah:

> *Let the wicked forsake his way, and the unrighteous man his thoughts; let him return to the Lord, that he may have compassion on him, and to our God, for he will abundantly pardon. For my thoughts are not your thoughts, neither are your ways my ways, declares the Lord. For as the heavens are higher than the earth, so are my ways higher than your ways and my thoughts than your thoughts (Isaiah 55:7–9 ESV).*

This is the essence of faith—the willingness to suspend the human reasoning of the moment and cling to the trustworthiness of Almighty God.

- **Life with God is hard. Life apart from God is dangerous.** In Chicago, where I live, the winter season is brutal and punishing. One of its enduring features is the constant sheet of ice blanketing driveways, sidewalks, and parkways. Every winter, victims stumble into emergency rooms with busted ankles and broken collarbones. This is what comes to my mind when I read Asaph's description of someone who attempts life without God. *He has set them on slippery places* (Psalm 73:18). I see someone striding across a dark, unsalted parking lot, dodging the lethal patches of dark ice that lurk beneath their shoes.

iFaith

In Chicago, we don't envy someone who has to navigate an unsalted lot, we pity them. At least I do. And so it is with those far from God. They shouldn't elicit our envy; they should provoke us to compassion. This is how God views them, not as enemies, but as people living on danger's edge.

- **God is better than your stuff.** In 2008, one of my childhood heroes, Michael Jordan, was elected to the Basketball Hall of Fame. As a teenager, I bought his shoes, tacked his poster on my wall, and watched every Bulls game. But when I tuned in for the induction ceremony, I was disappointed to hear what I perceived as the empty bitterness of a man who once held the world in the palm of his hand.

  It was a stark reminder that life without God is empty at best. Unlimited money, the applause of the crowd, and the worldwide fame do nothing to satiate a thirsty soul. Without God, you have nothing. With God, Asaph learned, you have everything you need.

- **We're not as good as we think we are.** Asaph entered the sanctuary of God assuming he was a pretty good guy. This happens to longtime believers. We start telling ourselves *I'm a pretty good guy. I'm doing so much for the Lord. I should be rewarded more. Where's the payoff?* I call this the martyr complex. We convince ourselves that we're doing so much, nobody else is doing anything, and that the entire plan of God rests on our giant shoulders. Asaph encountered a healthy dose of reality. *"God is the strength of my heart,"* he says (Psalm 73:26 ESV). The naked truth is that God's kingdom wasn't dependent on Asaph's noble service.

Today it's not dependent on Dan Darling's noble service. Each of us is a sinner redeemed by a merciful God and to serve Him is a privilege. The quicker we come to grips with who we really are, the quicker our doubts will melt into celebration of God's mercy on our behalf.

Questions

- Why are we so reticent to take our fears, doubts, and questions before God? Do we think He'll punish us for our honesty?
- In what way have your prayers become formulaic?
- What can we learn from the brave prayer life of Asaph?
- What promises of God seem upside down in your world?
- How does your time in God's sanctuary change your perspective on those seeming injustices?

Resources

- One of my favorite authors and pastors, Joshua Harris, has a terrific message on Psalm 73. You can find a complete archive of his sermons on his church's Web site: covlife.org.
- I also learned much from Bob Deffinbaugh's excellent message titled "Psalm 73: The Suffering of the Righteous and the Success of Sinners" at bible.org.
- You might also check out my article on Crosswalk .com titled, "Is God Fair? Maybe Not, But He's Right."

Bible

- Psalm 73
- 1 Peter 5:7
- Isaiah 32
- Hebrews 4

blue-screen faith
The Impossible Prayer

But let him ask in faith, with no doubting, for the one who doubts is like a wave of the sea that is driven and tossed by the wind.
—James 1:6 (ESV)

And without faith it is impossible to please him, for whoever would draw near to God must believe that he exists and that he rewards those who seek him.
—Hebrews 11:6 (ESV)

God's I AM is perfectly adequate for man's "I am not."
—Dr. Warren Wiersbe

When much of your life depends on a silver plastic box built by so-and-so, you can't afford a morning like the one I had a few years go.

After stumbling downstairs and chugging down a diet soda (don't tell me, I know diet soda will melt my brain), I flipped open my laptop to be greeted by the one thing every laptop user sweats—the blue screen of death. I had three really bad options.

- Reboot.
- Call tech support.
- Hope the local geek-for-hire could resuscitate it without draining my bank account.

There is really never a good time to be visited by the blue screen. But it *really* picked a bad time that morning.

I was in the midst of three overlapping jobs. I was the managing editor for an evangelical media ministry; I was working on my first book; and just for fun, I was the volunteer pro-life liaison for an important congressional race in my district.

Every one of those jobs demanded my laptop. So I spent the entire day on the phone with a less-than-helpful, difficult-to-understand tech support guy. Round and round we went through the same set of scripted procedures, only to come back each time with the blue screen of death.

When I called a local computer repair shop, the guy suggested I chuck the laptop and start over. But I didn't want to chuck the laptop and start over. I had all my work on there. Plus I was too cheap to buy a new one.

So, one more time, I punched in the now-memorized 800-number for tech support. This time I was miraculously connected to a level-two support professional. Besides being thoroughly competent, he was a Christ follower. He and I walked through several new procedures to try to save my computer.

Finally, after both of us had nearly given up, the

computer abandoned the blue and flickered to life. Everything was right in my world once again.

Life's Blue Screen

Maybe you've never been visited by the blue screen of death. Maybe you're not as attached to your laptop as I am. Perhaps you think I'm being slightly melodramatic.

But I'm guessing that you've had some blue-screen moments when the computer screen of your life screamed, "Impossible!"

I think of the dear sweet Christian woman who goes home every night to an abusive spouse and a disabled son. For 15 years she's endured his assaults, mostly verbal, sometimes physical, always cutting. She faithfully reads the Word every day and attends church as her husband allows. She does her best to serve her husband, knowing that he may never join her in faith. She stares at the impossible every single day.

I think of a young Christian executive who took a pay cut to resuscitate a sinking Christian ministry recently racked by scandal. Around him is the wreckage of the previous administration: a razor-thin budget, a shell-shocked staff, and eroding trust in the community. He left his safe corporate job because he strongly believes in the mission statement of this organization. Yet every day he feels a bit like Gideon leading a ragtag army.

For the middle-aged mother and grandmother, it's the stunning news her doctor delivers after a routine physical. After a lifetime of comforting, praying over, and physically assisting cancer patients, she is now in the crosshairs of this destructive disease. It's one thing to offer support. It's quite another to hear the C word attached to her name. She experiences the wide range of emotions, from dog-tired fatigue after chemo treatments to an overwhelming sense of hopelessness as the medical bills pile up.

I think of the struggling addict, who wakes up on Friday morning craving another high. His life is littered with the consequences: a shattered marriage and children who despise him. Addiction is the only life he's ever known. Now a believer, he keeps reading about spiritual victory, but it seems impossible. Every day is a struggle just to survive.

Your struggle may not be as dramatic or public, but each of us faces our own specialized blue screen, as we consider the gap between God's high calling and our own weakness.

When God's Equipping Meets Our Inadequacy

A few years ago, the blue screen hit me big time. Crosswinds of change swirled through my life. They were good changes, ones I had long dreamed and prayed and worked for. My family was growing; I was beginning my pastoral ministry; and new avenues were opening in my writing ministry.

Still, life seemed way too big for my abilities. God had placed me in unique positions of influence, authority, and responsibility, and so the inevitable doubts circulated in my head. *I can't do this. I'll find a way to mess this up. I'm not like those other guys.*

During this time God brought me a refreshing resource. A friend suggested Dr. Henry Blackaby's remarkable classic, *Experiencing God Day by Day.* So I began the year journaling through this book as part of my daily time with God.

The May 4 entry was a wonderful balm for my rising unbelief. Dr. Blackaby writes, "God uses our activities and circumstances to bring us to Himself. When He gives us a God-sized assignment, its sheer impossibility brings us back to Him for His enabling."

This was a lightbulb moment for me. It suddenly occurred to me that God purposely gave me assignments way bigger than my human capacity to perform them. Why? So I'd come to grips with my own frailty and lean in on the power of God.

WHY?

Curious, I started retracing the familiar stories from Scripture I'd learned since childhood. I realized that God sent His called-out children on a collision course with the impossible:

- God placed Moses between the banks of the mighty Red Sea and the approaching Egyptian cavalry.
- God placed David, the unknown shepherd boy, before the ruthless giant Goliath, armed only with a big faith and five small stones.
- God placed Deborah as a prophetess and judge in a nation devoid of spiritual leaders and fearful of the enemy.
- God gave Gideon only 300 men in his battle with the mighty Midianite army.

- God called the impoverished teenage Mary to carry the Messiah in her womb.

When we're in an impossible situation, our default position is to think of the Red Seas, the Goliaths, and the Gideon armies as bizarre twists of fate in an unfair world. Even Christ followers tend to doubt God can do the impossible. Faced with a blue screen, we shrink back in unbelief.

The only way we dial back that fear is to realize that God's impossible callings are not random, cosmic missteps, but opportunities for growth. They are faith-building exercise by a God who takes supreme delight in our humble, weak, but dependent faith (Hebrews 11:6).

But What Is Faith?

Faith, then, is the key that unlocks the door of heaven; that invites the power of God into our lives. Writing to a first-century church bombarded by opposition, persecution, and inadequacy, James said:

But let him ask in faith, with no doubting, for the one who doubts is like a wave of the sea that is driven and tossed by the wind.
—James 1:6 (ESV)

In his book *How to Keep Your Inner Mess from Trashing Your Outer World*, author and pastor Bill Giovenetti writes:

> *A holy life is a mighty struggle.... But it is not the struggle you think it is. It is not a struggle to imitate Christ directly or do good works or*

produce holiness, or subdue passions.... The real struggle is the struggle to believe. Fight the fight of faith. As often as you win that battle, all other victories fall into place.

Faith puts you in the driver's seat and it makes your Inner Mess shut up and go for the ride. Faith puts you in full possession of your faculties. It activates the power of Christ, responds to his Lordship, and puts you in fellowship with the Spirit.

But What Does This Faith Look Like?

Faith can refer to a set of religious beliefs. People often talk of the Jewish faith or the Muslim faith or the Christian faith. And in the Scriptures, sometimes the entirety of biblical doctrine is summed up as "the faith" (Jude 1:3).

Faith can also mean confidence. When I sit in my dentist's chair, I have faith he won't drill through my gums and into my brain. When I drive on Chicago's icy winter roads, I have faith the combination of my skillful driving (Angela begs to differ), the car's antilock breaking system, and the requisite salt on the pavement will carry me safely to my destination. When I turn on WGN radio in the summer, I have faith (misplaced) that the Chicago Cubs will finally win a World Series.

But what is the faith that so pleases God and unlocks the flow of His power? The clearest definition is found in a unique chapter, what is often called the faith chapter, Hebrews 11. The very first verse defines faith: "*Now faith is the substance of things hoped for, the evidence of things not seen*" (Hebrews 11:1 KJV).

In other words, the faith that pleases God is not necessarily a set of beliefs, though what you believe does matter. Nor is faith about *what* you do or *how hard* you do it.

The Bible simply says faith is believing in something, or rather, Someone you can't see. It is entrusting the totality of your life to an unseen power. In this case, Jesus Christ.

Then the author takes the reader on a journey through the lives of some of the most colorful characters in the Old Testament Scriptures. He illustrates faith on the movie screen of their lives, showing us what faith looks like in blue jeans and flannel shirts, in board meetings and conference calls, in living rooms and minivans.

The Man Who Said Amen

Nobody's story garners more ink on in Hebrews chapter of faith than one man—the Hebrew patriarch, Abraham. He is put forward as the Bible's preeminent man of faith.

Hebrews isn't alone in its assessment of Abraham. Consider how others in the Scripture viewed him:

- In His earthly ministry, Jesus pointed to the faith of Abraham (John 8:56).
- Stephen, the first martyr of the early church, acknowledged Abraham's faith (Acts 7:1–8).
- The Apostle Paul acknowledged his faith (Romans 4:3).
- James, the resident leader of the church at Jerusalem, acknowledged Abraham's faith (James 2:23).

If Noah was known for the ark and Jonah for the whale and David for Goliath and Joshua for crumbling walls and Moses for a Red Sea, then Abraham is known for faith.

In fact, the very first mention of the word *faith* in the Bible is used in association with Abraham in Genesis 15:6. The original Hebrew word has the same root as the word *amen*. It means that Abraham put his full weight on the promises of God. Abraham said amen to God.

I like what Paul said about Abraham's faith. "*He staggered not at the promise of God through unbelief; but was strong in faith, giving glory to God; And being fully persuaded that, what he had promised, he was able also to perform*" (Romans 4:20–21 KJV).

He staggered not, possessed no unbelief, was strong in faith, and was fully persuaded. Wow. Was this guy Superman or something? Did he possess a supernatural gift we mere mortals can only envy?

Ur was New York City.

Well, when you investigate Abraham's life story, told in great detail in Genesis, you realize he was flesh and blood like you and me. Here was a man who lied twice about his wife, had a child with his handmaid, and laughed at God.

So we know Abraham wasn't perfect. But what was it about his faith that made God so happy and unlocked God's power in his life?

Blue-Screen Faith Is Uncomfortable

When God first came to him, Abraham was living the good life. He was set to inherit his father's great wealth;

he was married to a lovely wife, Sarah; and he lived in the comfortable urban environment of Ur. Ur was the New York City of Mesopotamia. Nestled along the Euphrates River, Ur was an economic engine and a cosmopolitan center of trade and commerce.

Abraham and Sarah were living the Mesopotamian version of the American dream—with one painful exception. They were unable to produce children.

Then one day the Lord showed up in Abraham's life with a risky venture. God was calling out a new people to form a new nation and wanted Abraham to be its father. The fame of Abraham, the Lord said, would spread through the land and echo through history.

But there was a catch. Abraham had to move from his life of ease and follow God into the great unknown. The details were vague, only *"go to the land that I will show you"* (Genesis 12:1). Hebrews 11:8 says that Abraham *"went out, not knowing where he was going."*

On the surface, Abraham's sojourn seems adventurous but not that risky, a bit like going off to college after high school. Plus, the members of our generation are mobile, willing to move from state to state to build a career.

But the call to Abraham was more than that. It was a major, life-altering decision. Bible scholars John Walton and Victor H. Matthews describe exactly what was at stake: "When Abram gave up his place in his father's household, he forfeited his security. He was putting his survival, his identity, his future and his security in the hands of the Lord."

God's call involved more questions than answers. How was Abraham supposed to build a great nation if he gave up his inheritance and left his family behind?

How would a family begin if Sarah's womb was closed?

None of it made sense. Yet, Abraham went.

That, right there, is the essence of faith.

To be sure, God isn't extending exactly the same invitation to you and to me as He did to Abraham, but He does call us to the same uncomfortable faith. He drags us from the ease of our American Christian life, pushing us to live above the level of mediocrity.

What I've learned from Abraham is that faith often isn't big, bold, or overly theological. Usually it's putting one foot in front of the other and obeying God.

God does His greatest work on the margins of comfort, when the impossibility of our calling collides with the reality of our human frailty.

The question is, are we willing to live the unsafe life? When presented with an opportunity like Abraham, are we willing to make that leap, without knowing where it will lead? Or are we satisfied with our spirituality doled out in manageable chunks, content to simply check off the right spiritual boxes and live safely?

Blue-Screen Faith
Is God-Centered Faith

It is easy to be intimidated by a man like Abraham, because his faith seems so strong and so powerful. But the real story here is not about Abraham; it's about God.

When God plucked Abraham from the comfort of Ur, his commitment seemed marginal. According to Stephen's account in Acts 7, God first called Abraham in his hometown of Ur. But when we find Abraham in Genesis 12, he is in Haran, a considerable distance from

Ur, but only halfway to Canaan. And in Haran, he was still living with his father.

This looks a lot like my spiritual journey, and perhaps it resembles yours. Few of us are willing or even ready to plunge head-first into the full spectrum of God's will immediately after salvation. Our faith is weak, our view of God is small. But God patiently works with us *where we are*. The psalmist writes that the Lord *"knows our frame and remembers we are dust"* (Psalm 103:14 ESV). Jesus told His disciples that they didn't need huge faith; they only needed mustard seed-sized faith (Matthew 17:20).

@

ABRAHAM TO LET GO.

It took a lifetime for God to stretch Abraham, gradually removing his comforts, stripping him of security, and forcing an ever-increasing dependence on Him.

Initially, Abraham's faith carried him only as far as Haran and he had to bring his father, but God called him to go farther and told him to leave his family behind (Genesis 12).

Abraham did go farther, but still brought his nephew, Lot, because perhaps God would need Lot to build that mighty nation. But eventually God took away Lot (Genesis 13).

Then Abraham suggested his servant, Eliezer, as the steward of the next generation. But God didn't need Eliezer to build a nation. He promised Abraham a son (Genesis 15).

Then, pressured by his wife, nervous of his advancing age, Abraham again tried to help God by having a son with Sarah's handmaid, Hagar (Genesis 16:1–4). He offered the son, Ishmael, to God as the way to build that new nation (Genesis 17:18). But God rejected Ishmael and once again affirmed His promise of a son through Sarah (Genesis 17:19–21).

Abraham didn't understand. Sarah laughed. But along the way their faith grew. That mustard seed nurtured into increasing fruitfulness by the patient hand of God. In each season of life, God stripped away a little more security and Abraham revealed a little more trust. He trusted God to provide land when Lot chose the most fertile acres (Genesis 13:8–18). He tithed a tenth of his possessions to Melchizedek, the high priest (Genesis 14:20). He refused the spoils of war, bowing to the providence of God (Genesis 14:20–24).

Eventually, God saw fit to change his name (Genesis 17), from Abram, "exalted one," to Abraham, "father of multitudes." The weak-kneed man of Ur was growing into a man of faith.

When Isaac was born, God's work in Abraham wasn't finished. Still to come was the epic test of Mt. Moriah. God asked Abraham to let go of his most precious possession, the son he had waited a lifetime to see.

You know the story. It is arguably the greatest example of faith in the Scriptures. Bigger than Job. Better than Daniel. More daring than Gideon. Here on Moriah, Abraham's trust in the Lord is breathtaking. We hear him whisper memorable, prophetic words as his son Isaac, lay on the altar. *"My son, God will provide himself a lamb"* (Genesis 22:8 KJV).

No longer was Abraham's commitment halfway, mediocre, risk-averse. It was a full-on, all-in faith. I imagine on Moriah, his mind played through the highlights of God's provision. If God could prosper Abraham in the wild-untamed Canaan, if God could rescue him twice from his own folly in Egypt, if God could provide a son from the barren womb of Sarah, surely God would provide a Lamb.

The story isn't about Abraham, though. The story is about God's work in the life of an average, everyday follower. And what God did in Abraham, God wants to do in you and me.

Our journey doesn't begin on Mt. Moriah, but back in Ur. God doesn't look for superheroes but fragile, faithless followers who offer only clumsy, halfway broken faith. If we're willing, He'll stretch that mustard seed into a mountain-moving faith.

The truth is that Abraham's life wasn't an unbroken line of obedience. In between those grand moments of faith, we find large swaths of unbelief.

And yet, when we arrive at the New Testament commentary on the life of Abraham, we find no record of Abraham's misdeeds. We only see his successes highlighted and his faith celebrated.

God always takes the long view, and the long arc of Abraham's life was one of dependence on the Lord.

We have no reason to think God would treat us any differently. We see through the lens of the daily microscope, all those panicky choices made in unbelief, the sin patterns, and the reactions made in the flesh.

But God looks beneath the layers of our humanity and looks for the mustard seed, the faith, and finds something He can grow to glorify Him.

The Daily Blue Screen

Every day we wake up to a fresh blue screen. The enemy flashes the impossibility of our calling, the sheer weight of what God has called us to. He carefully edits out the part about God's power and God's enabling.

And so, every day we're faced with a choice. We can shrink back in fear or we can hold onto the hope that God can take sin-soaked, faithless sinners like you and like me and use us to accomplish His purpose.

From a worldly, horizontal perspective, it's impossible, it's illogical, and it's foolish. And yet every day we must believe God can do the impossible through us, because it is faith that unlocks the power of God, and it is unbelief that opens the door to sin and failure.

My friend, author and pastor Ray Pritchard, says, "When your God is big, your view of yourself will be small enough that you won't stoop to foolish deception as a way of life. It is only when your God is too small that you are forced to compromise your standards."

Our biggest problem is not that we're not trying hard enough or that we're not doing enough for God. Our biggest problem is that our faith is too small. We fear that if we follow God, somehow we'll mess up and He'll crush us and take us off His program.

That's why the most important prayer we pray every day is not, *"Lead us not into temptation,"* or *"Help me to live right,"* but the prayer of the father who asked Jesus for a miracle. *"Lord, I believe; help my unbelief"* (Mark 9:24 ESV).

Ephesians 6 says that the first weapon we pick up is the shield of faith. *You have to believe* that you can do what God has set before you.

Questions

- Describe some blue screens (impossible situations) you face in your life. Why do you think God has allowed you to face those? What is God trying to teach you in these impossible moments?
- Why is Abraham held up as the model of faith in the Scriptures?
- Describe some instances in which God stripped away Abraham's security in order to grow his faith. What are some ways God is stretching you?
- Why is belief our biggest daily struggle?
- Why is faith the most important aspect of prayer? What prayer should we pray every day?

Resources

- My good friend Pastor Bill Giovenetti has written a powerful book, *How to Keep Your Inner Mess from Trashing Your Outer World*. This book really clarified the inner struggle Paul describes in Romans 6–8. Bill uses descriptive, powerful language.
- There are some really great books on the life of Abraham, but none better, in my mind than F. B. Meyer's *The Obedience of Faith*.

Bible

- Genesis 11–25
- Acts 7
- Romans 4
- Galatians 6
- James 2:20–24
- Hebrews 7, 11

reboot your life
The Message in the Meltdown

Elijah was a man with a nature like ours.
—James 5:17 (ESV)

There are times when God's work demands strenuous action. And there is a time when you need to sit in the recliner, crank it back, get a bowl of Cheetos and a Coke, pick up the remote control, and watch ESPN for a while.
—Ray Pritchard

It was easily the most boring class I ever attended—Basic Computer Skills. The teacher might have been a qualified expert on the inner workings of a PC, but his skills as an orator made Al Gore look like Billy Mays. I'd probably hire him to fix my laptop, but I'm sticking forks in my eye any time he's speaking in public.

Captain Charisma's class wasn't a total loss, though, because I did leave with one important lesson: When all else fails and your computer is operating slower than me pushing a vacuum, there is only one thing to do.

Reboot.

It's actually good advice. Computer nerds will tell you that periodic refreshing of the system is healthy for long-term viability.

Not sure why it took a 30-minute class to explain it, though.

Reboot Your Life

I'm finding that rebooting is essential for the long-term viability of the soul. We're enmeshed in a harried, busy culture. Pick up a business or leadership magazine and you'll read glowing profiles of successful people. One common thread is that these guys climbed the ladder by working insanely long hours. Sleeping at the office is a virtue. I read recently about one NFL coach who arrives at the training facility at 6:00 A.M. on "normal" weekdays and 4:00 A.M. during playoff weeks.

And it's not just about "going home," because when we finally go home, are we really home? That's a point my wife consistently makes: "You're here," she says, "but you're not really here."

Last year we embarked on a family "cation" (my five-year-old daughter, Grace's, word for getting away). Inevitably, I found myself glued to the iPhone. As we walked in the Blue Ridge Mountains or relaxed on the sands of Myrtle Beach, there I was, scrolling through emails, checking Facebook, texting an idea to a friend or church leader. On more than one occasion Angela threatened to toss the phone out the car window. One of these days she'll make good on that threat.

An Old Testament Superhero

As I've struggled with the work/life balance, I've struggled to find an apt example in the Scriptures of today's busy believer. I kept coming back to Elijah. He lived centuries before the age of technology, but his hard-charging, full-throttle personality would fit perfectly in today's church. Elijah was a ball of energy, a one-man endorsement for energy drinks, a hairy-chested, muscled biblical superhero.

Elijah was a man of Gilead, the rugged mountainous region in modern-day Jordan. Gilead didn't produce latte-sipping, sandal-wearing, pedicure-receiving guys. They produced rough-and-tumble guys with an edge to them.

God brought Elijah into Israel at just the right time. His energy and passion for God was exactly the leader God's people needed to awaken them from their spiritual lethargy. King Ahab and his aggressive wife, Jezebel, were successfully leading the nation away from worship of the true God and toward worship of the pagan gods, Baal and Asherah.

Elijah stirred Israel with bold, spirit-filled preaching. Like his New Testament counterpart John the Baptist, the prophet passionately spoke truth to power. For three-and-a-half years, Elijah was a one-man revolution, the chief thorn in the side of Israel's ruling establishment.

- He correctly prophesied a country-wide famine, proving that the true God and not Baal held the spigots of heaven, bringing Israel's agrarian economy to a halt (1 Kings 17:1).

- He dared the practitioners of Baal worship to a contest on Mt. Carmel, calling down fire from heaven in a breathtaking display of God's power (1 Kings 18:1–40).

- He prayed and called down rain from heaven again as God halted the famine in Israel (1 Kings 18:41–45).

Elijah was a spiritual *tour de force* single-handedly leading a nationwide revival. But while Israel needed revival, Elijah needed renewal.

Most Christians are familiar with the dramatic story of his exploits on Mt. Carmel, but few know Elijah's full story—how a national hero suddenly retreated in fear to the backside of nowhere, despondent and lonely. It doesn't quite fit our tidy narrative of a Bible superhero. But James knew. This pastor and apostle reminds us that Elijah was a man with *"a nature like ours"* (James 5:17 ESV). In his commentary on James's words, Dr. Harry Ironside suggests, "We are apt to think of prophets and other servants of God mentioned in the Bible as men who were of a different fiber than we are. But they were all of the same family of frail humanity."

The Valley After the Mountain

We see Elijah's "frail humanity" in full color when we crack open the 19th chapter of 1 Kings. Here our Bible superhero is in a surprisingly desperate condition.

Just days before, Elijah was the spiritual conscience of a nation, the bold leader who pulled God's people back from the brink of judgment. His encounter with

Baal on Mt. Carmel drove a stake into the heart of Israel's idolatry by exposing Baal as a fraud, a dead god, an imposter. In those heady moments, Elijah uttered one of the Bible's most memorable lines. *"How long will you go limping between two different opinions? If the Lord is God, follow him; but if Baal, then follow him"* (1 Kings 18:21 ESV).

So, you would assume Elijah spent the next several days glowing in the aftermath of a hard-fought victory. Wasn't this a time to celebrate? But when we flip the page in Elijah's biography, we find something entirely different.

Gone is the fearless prophet.

Gone is the man of unquestioned faith.

Gone is the spiritual superhero.

In his place is a weeping, despondent, suicidal shell of a man. If it wasn't written in the black and white of Scripture, we'd never believe it. This can't possibly be the rough-and-tumble, bullet-proof prophet we know from Mt. Carmel.

From Courage to Fear

When you see Elijah living desperately under that juniper tree, the first question that comes to mind is, *What happened?*

What triggered this sudden, deep-down depression? On the surface, everything seemed fine. Israel repented; the prophets of Baal were destroyed; the Lord was worshipped; and it started raining. I mean Eljiah even outran Ahab's chariot.

Isn't that enough to make a prophet happy?

But then we peel back the layers of Elijah's life and the cracks begin to show. There was the constant threat of Queen Jezebel, whose heart was colder than a Chicago winter. While all of Israel fell on their knees before the true God, her heart was unfazed by God's vivid demonstration of power. Jezebel reacted by threatening Elijah's life, sending an ominous letter by courier. I imagine the color drained from Elijah's face as he read her words. They were the cruel drops of cold water on Israel's God-parade. All the successes Elijah witnessed on Mt. Carmel now faded into the background. For Elijah, the joy of Mt. Carmel was no match for the agony of Jezebel's stubborn rejection.

I can understand Elijah, even in a small way. I'm not comparing myself to the prophet, by any stretch. I've never prophesied or called down rain from heaven. And I can't even outrun my daughter's tricycle. Yet as a pastor, I have experienced the surge of disappointment that always seems to greet me after a great spiritual victory. If every Sunday is Mt. Carmel, many Mondays are soaked with the cool rains of Jezebel discouragements.

You may not be in ministry, but I'm sure you've felt the crushing weight of defeat, days after experiencing a spiritual high with the Lord. Perhaps you've attended a life-changing conference only to go home and have your passion snuffed out by a negative, carnal church member. Or maybe you've witnessed a powerful conversion to Christianity by someone you've long prayed over. Then you see that person slip into old ways of sin and your heart is broken.

One thing we know. It seems that small hurts can overshadow big victories in the recesses of the human heart.

From Fear to Grace

I believe God allowed Elijah to suffer this discouragement for a purpose, because He wanted to correct a fatal flaw in his theology.

Elijah bought into a common spiritual myth. It plagues believers today. I call it the superhero mentality. Others have labeled it the missionary mind-set or the martyr complex.

It's the mistaken idea that activity *for* God is a worthy substitute for intimacy *with* God. We take responsibility for outcomes and results, and convince ourselves that normal, human weaknesses shouldn't apply to Christians.

Truthfully, I see a lot of the superhero mentality in myself. Granted, I'll never be the raw, Baal-challenging, never-say-die prophet Elijah was. Actually, I sip lattes, attend Weight Watchers, and prefer to hunt my meat at the local supermarket.

But like Elijah I often live as if God's entire plan depends on my working another 16-hour day at church or pounding out another Christian book or scheduling another ministry meeting.

Often God has to allow us to arrive at the juniper tree—desperate, despondent, and discouraged. We have to come to the end of our strength.

Then He is there to receive with grace another burned-out prophet.

Pizza over Prayer

What exactly was God's cure for Elijah's superhero mentality?

Another Bible study?

Another Christian bestseller?

Another three-day seminar?

Those are things we'd suggest. And we have the four-color brochures to prove it! But God didn't tell Elijah to pray more, read more Scriptures, or build an altar.

No, God did something so practical that it almost seems unbiblical. He brought food. Not stale cafeteria sandwiches or day-old carryout either.

God provided a fresh, four-course meal, cooked to perfection in the kitchens of heaven and delivered directly to Elijah's shade-tree motel.

When was the last time Elijah had eaten? I'm guessing he skipped a few meals because he had "important ministry to do." *How can you stop for a hamburger when the world needs to be saved?*

But the Creator of the heavens and the earth, who had lovingly fashioned Elijah's body to be nourished and rested, knew better. And after Elijah polished off that meal, guess what God did? He brought another meal.

I think there is an important lesson here. You don't even need a seminary degree to discover it. It's this: sometimes pizza is more important than prayer.

We have to come to grips with a sobering reality. It's really not God's will for us to live like we're superhuman. God delights in our humanity. He shines in our weakness. His glory is revealed when we desperately lean on Him for strength.

I'm reminded of the words of the psalmist, who writes, "He knows our frame; remembers that we are dust" (Psalm 103:14 ESV). God remembers we're dust, but we often forget.

Perhaps, because we live in an evangelical culture that is in love with benchmarks to tell us how good we're doing spiritually, we are compelled to create our handy lists, which vary from church tradition to church tradition, denomination to denomination. But doesn't weakness, the human inability to produce anything good, lie at the very heart of the gospel message?

We have to ask ourselves, *Are we really doing God a favor by neglecting the normal, natural care of our bodies?* We have to take a close look at our theology. Is it man-centered and performance-based? Do we really think God sits aloft in heaven, crossing His fingers, hoping one more saint puts in a 16-hour day?

God allowed Elijah's meltdown, so He could pour into him an important truth that would revitalize Elijah's life and equip him for years of fruitful ministry. *God wasn't dependent on Elijah; God wanted Elijah dependent upon Him.*

Under that shade tree, Elijah was no longer the superhero. He was helpless. He was weak. He was exactly where God wanted him.

REST.

The shade tree is where we find the solution to some of our deepest problems: rest. None of us is above the natural breaking down of our bodies. None of us is so special that we can escape the effect of the demanding lives we live. None of us is superhuman.

It's ironic that we confuse busyness for God with connection with God, foolishly dismissing as unspiritual the necessary elements of nourishment and rest. We've allowed a false view of God to guilt us out of necessary relaxation, rest, and soul care.

Maybe because we've always heard how urgent it is to get out there and win the world for Christ. *How can you sit on your couch when the world is going to hell? The devil doesn't take vacation. We can rest in heaven.*

That sounds so spiritual and maybe it earns a few more points with the legalists. But the real truth is that weakness is an intrinsic aspect of our humanity. Even Jesus, the perfect God-man, prioritized rest. On more than one occasion, He retreated from ministry demands and escaped to a quiet place.

The superhero syndrome is typical of new believers. I see it every year. A person comes to faith in Christ, experiences radical heart change, and dives head-first into Jesus. In our desire to see this new disciple grow, we dump a million spiritual to-dos on him. Soon he's racing through church life at breakneck speed.

Then, one day you look up and that fresh-faced new Christ follower is gone. He doesn't show up at church. He doesn't return your calls. He slinks into the abyss of uselessness where the enemy loves to entertain.

Most observers bemoan his fate, chalking it up to something like, "Well, his faith didn't really take root."

But maybe it wasn't that at all. Maybe he learned how to get really busy *for* God, but didn't really learn how to take time to stay connected *to* God.

I believe Elijah's story allows us to vividly see the inescapable link between the physical and the spiritual and to come to grips with our human limitations. Fatigue, hunger, and pain can seriously cloud our judgment, dull our senses, and set us up for an Elijah-like meltdown.

Rebooting Your Life

When Elijah finally did speak, you can almost hear the whine. *God, I've done all of this great stuff here. I'm working very hard for You. And look what happened. Jezebel rebelled. I'm the only one standing up for You. Can You help me out here?*

Instead of answering Elijah directly, God answered him with a dramatic illustration. He told Elijah to stand and watch. In a matter of minutes, there were three powerful natural manifestations of God's power: fire, wind, and an earthquake. But Scripture tells us that God was not *in* any of these.

Does this mean God was powerless over nature? No, the Scriptures overwhelmingly affirm God as the all-powerful Creator (Genesis 1–2; Job 38–39; John 1; Colossians 1; Hebrews 1). So what is God saying to Elijah and to us?

The same message shared in Psalm 46:10: *"Be still and know that I am God."* God doesn't need wind and fire and earthquake to be God. God doesn't need megachurches, best-selling book tours, and stadium-sized rallies to be God. God speaks in the quiet. His Spirit is like the soft wind of a gentle breeze.

@

"Be still . . ."

Elijah's story caused me to reconsider my approach to spirituality. Like Elijah, I've often arrived at the margins of my physical strength, feeling alone and without hope. And yet it has been those moments of utter humanity, when my spiritual mask is removed, that God meets me in my weakness.

I'm reminded just who is human and who is God. I'm stripped of my self-imposed standards for success. I realize that God isn't always in the big, powerful movements where men are tempted to beat their chests in pride. But God is active in the stillness of the gentle breezes of life. If only I'm weak enough to listen.

The Elijah that emerged from the wilderness was new and different and humble. Years of fruitfulness followed. God used him to shape the next generation of spiritual leadership in Israel (2 Kings 2:1–8). He saw the house of Ahab fall (1 Kings 22). He gained a grand entrance into heaven (2 Kings 2:9–17).

When we grasp this message, when we fall back in despair on the arms of the Lord, like Elijah, we'll be spiritually tuned for the long haul, for a balanced, effective life of service. Because the story won't be about us and our greatness, but about God and His glory.

Questions

- In what ways does your life resemble the full-throttle, no-rest lifestyle of Elijah? How are you depending on your own strength instead of God's?
- How can you build rest into your schedule? What good, but not great, things can you eliminate from your life in order to give your body and soul a chance to breathe?
- Why is the martyr complex so inviting? What negative character traits does it reveal from your heart?
- How has God met you in your weaknesses?

Resources

- Ray Pritchard has a fantastic series of sermons on the life of Elijah on his Web site, keepbelieving.com. He's also written a terrific book, *Fire and Rain, the Wildhearted Faith of Elijah.*
- I can't recommend more highly *Liberating Ministry from the Success Syndrome*, by Dr. R. Kent Hughes and his wife, Barbara.
- John Ortberg wrote a terrific article in the Winter edition of *Leadership Journal* titled, "Your Spiritual Growth Plan."
- Kay Arthur has written a terrific piece for Crosswalk. com titled, "Why I Stopped Striving."

Bible

- 1 Kings 17–21
- 2 Kings 1–2
- Malachi 4
- Matthew 17:1–13
- Mark 9:2–13
- Luke 9:28–36
- James 5:17–18
- Romans 11:2

the world's first prayer meeting

Prayer and Faith in an Age of Progress

*And he told them a parable to the effect
that they ought always to pray and not lose heart.*
—Luke 18:1 (ESV)

*Prayer is the mightiest agent to advance God's work.
Praying hearts and hands only can do God's work.
Prayer succeeds when all else fails.
Prayer has won great victories, and rescued, with notable triumph,
God's saints when every other hope was gone.
Men who know how to pray are the greatest boon God can give
    to earth—they are the richest gift earth can offer heaven.*
—E. M. Bounds

On Sunday evening, February 4, 2007, I made a grown man cry.

A group of friends were gathered at our house in the Chicago suburbs, every eye fixed on the first play of the Super Bowl as our beloved Bears faced the Indianapolis Colts. Chicago's best player, Devin Hester, was cracking off a 92-yard kickoff return when my television turned from FOX to fuzz.

When Hester began his run back, my spry-but-60-year-old friend Dave leaped off the couch in excitement, shaking the ground and rattling the cable on the back of the TV, just enough to dislodge it. Rather than witness the touchdown; I was scrambling like a mad scientist to put the cord back in its place. Dave, still living the glory days of 1985, exchanged his calm Christian demeanor for something resembling a monster.

That night ended up in disaster for the Bears as they fumbled and stumbled their way to a 29-17 drubbing. But the night was not a total loss.

At the end of the game, the eyes of the world were on Coach Tony Dungy, who finally silenced his critics and won a Lombardi Trophy. What would he say? Would he give the standard coach-speak? *We have the greatest fans. It's all on the players. We had a plan going into training camp and we executed it. This is what we came to do.*

Dungy surprised everyone. When the announcer shoved a mike in his face and asked, "How do you feel, Coach?" the first thing Dungy mentioned was his faith. Apparently this was the message he considered most important to share with 90 million or so people.

And he didn't share the gospel in the typical, pointing-to-the-sky, I-just-want-to-give-all-the-glory-to-God way we have come to expect from athletes—hackneyed Christian pabulum we ignore.

No, this accomplished, now Super Bowl-winning coach used this enormous, once-in-a-lifetime platform to share an authentic message of gratitude to his Savior. I still remember watching him, forgetting my allegiance to Chicago and welling up with pride that Tony Dungy first represented another kind of team. A team I belonged to. God's team. The church.

In that moment it was clear what was truly important to the Super Bowl-winning coach of the Indianapolis Colts. It wasn't winning an NFL championship. It was representing his God before the world's single largest audience.

In a profile with the *Florida Baptist Witness*, Eva Wolever explains that Dungy's faith is a hallmark of his life:

> *Dungy told about a job interview in which his prospective employer asked him if the job would be the most important thing in his life. Dungy said he told the man, "No." "I didn't think I was going to get that job, and I didn't," Dungy said, laughing. "For your faith to be more important than your job, for your family to be more important than your job, it's things we all talk about, we all know that's the way it should be, but we're afraid to say that sometimes."*

I find Dungy's perspective refreshing, but astonishingly rare, even among self-proclaimed Christians.

Progressing Away from Faith

Few of us will stand on a podium and speak to a rapt audience of 90 million. Few will have the opportunity and platform of a Coach Tony Dungy. And yet, I wonder if we pass up similar opportunities in the smaller arenas in which we live and work.

It's become natural in our progressive age to crowd out God in the daily flow of life. We go to church; we attend a small group; and we even serve in a leadership capacity in a local church. And yet when the rubber meets the road, devotion is becoming increasingly marginalized in favor of other, more exciting pursuits. Even pastors aren't immune. A recent survey by LifeWay Research reveals that 39 percent of evangelical *pastors* spend only four hours a week in personal prayer and Bible study.

What's interesting is that our decline in piety is coming at a time when the opportunity to connect with God has never been easier. We have unlimited spiritual resources at our fingertips. You can't walk into a department store without passing aisles of Christian books and Bibles. Even my local home improvement store has an inspirational section.

You can go online and read the Bible in any language or version. There is a seemingly unlimited supply of Bible study resources, devotionals, commentaries, language dictionaries—all free and all online. We have the Bible on our cell phones. We podcast sermons and download Christian music. Churches everywhere host conferences and Bible studies nearly every weekend of the year in almost every corner of our country. You can even pursue advanced theological education from your home online, 24 hours a day.

In spite of increased opportunity, anecdotally and statistically, God's people seem less biblically literate, less prayerful, and less connected to the faith.

I wonder if our prosperous, technology-driven life is part of the problem. We live in the most progressive society in the history of civilization. Communication, travel, medicine, science, and technology have given us a false sense of control over our environment. Prosperity and choice and freedom have unburdened us from the daily struggles of people in Third-World countries. And so in this enlightened age, we have convinced ourselves that we're really OK; we're in control; and we really don't need God anymore.

It Began . . . In the Beginning

But before you sell your laptop and go live in the forest, you need to know that our drift away from God is nothing new. Progress in society has always had an uneasy relationship with spirituality. Just read the Old Testament and you'll discover this to be the natural cycle of humanity.

Consider the very first civilization. Adam and Eve were birthed in innocence and placed in the pristine environment of the Garden of Eden, the ideal environment for creativity, intimacy with God, and growth. God shared a unique relationship with His prized creation, granting Adam stewardship over all of creation.

OUR DRIFT AWAY FROM GOD IS NOTHING NEW.

But an adversary lurked in the shadows, ready to pounce on the innocence of Adam and strike a blow to the heart of God. Isaiah 14:12-23 describes the foolish hubris of Lucifer, the one-time prince of heaven, who declared himself a god and demanded equality with the Trinity. Lucifer took a third of the angel host with him and commenced a history-long agenda to defeat God. Lucifer, now Satan, couldn't rule heaven, so he poured out his wrath on God's highest creation, man, given a free will by God. Man could choose to love or choose to rebel against God's created order.

Alas, if the Bible ended at Genesis 2, it would be a short story. We'd still be living naked and innocent in a lush garden environment. I wouldn't be trudging through deep Chicago snow and whining about high taxes and corruption.

But there is much more to this story. One chapter later, we come face-to-face with the root cause of a society's ills, both ancient and modern. Inhabiting the sleek body of a serpent, Satan perverted God's truth and tempted Adam and Eve to sin against God.

According to Romans 5:12, this seemingly harmless moment was the seminal event of history. By one man sin entered the world, and death by sin, so that death passed upon all people.

But the Godhead wasn't caught flat-footed by sin's introduction into the created order. A plan was already in place for the redemption and rescue of mankind. God's words of rebuke to the adversary foretold a violent struggle between the two rivals, a struggle God won in the death and resurrection of the Son, Jesus Christ.

Two Divergent Paths

Satan's lusty offer made sin seem harmless, even fun. But sin was anything but fun. It began a violent course through the human race, inflicting permanent damage after only one generation.

The fourth chapter of Genesis shares the well-known story of Cain and Abel. More than a sibling rivalry, Cain and Abel are symbols of the violent struggle between God and Satan.

Each represents one of two ways to approach God. Abel approached as a repentant worshipper, offering the sacrifice of an innocent one as a covering for sin. Cain came religiously; proud of the works his hands produced.

Abel embodies the theology of Calvary, where sinners find the ultimate covering for their sin in the shed blood of an innocent Lamb. Cain personifies the theology of the serpent, a monument to the perceived righteousness of self.

Today, the world is divided into the sphere of Abel and the sphere of Cain. On one side are those willing to bow their knee to the Lamb, acknowledging their sin and need for atonement. On the other side stand the sons of Cain, armed with their self-righteousness, convinced their goodness will merit a hearing from the Almighty.

CAIN PERSONIFIES THE THEOLOGY OF THE SERPENT.

God rejected Cain's offering because God's favor couldn't be earned by the sweat of a man's hands. He informed him that sin, like a tiger, crouched at the door of his heart (Genesis 4:6–8).

Cain rejected God's entreaties of grace, and sin festered and grew until his brother lay dead in a pool of blood. God's pronounced punishment for Cain was to curse the ground. The land would no longer yield its beauty for this confessed murderer.

But rather than fall in humble repentance and dependence upon the Almighty, Cain turned his bloody hands toward another profession. Cain became the world's first city builder.

The World's First City

As a lifelong Chicagoan, I've become a bit of a local history buff. Our fair city has a rich history of intrigue, corruption, and progress.

Cities are amazing wonders created by man. Each is an amazing feat of engineering and skill, leveraging complex water systems, transportation grids, technology, and architecture. The pulse of each city beats with a certain vibe, a unique mix of ethnic sensibilities, imported culture, and bustling commerce.

Man has always prided himself on the building of cities, from Nebuchadnezzar's hanging gardens to Herod's impressive infrastructure to the still marvelous structures that attract tourists to the ancient cities across Europe and Asia.

But the first city was built by Cain and his descendants. Cain's line built an impressive civilization. Genesis describes the progress that occurred. Each generation advanced with new technologies. Scripture and recent archeological discoveries reveal this society to be a pioneer in the domestication of animals and the practices of metallurgy. Creativity flowed from generation to generation, with a full-orbed development of the arts and music, including the invention of instruments still popular today.

Decades of evolutionary theory have mistakenly led us to believe that people in ancient times were all brutish and stupid, living in caves and rubbing rocks together. But the biblical account and archeological evidence reveals that these were extremely brilliant, creative, and inventive people.

And yet, not unlike the cities today, the world's first

city advanced, but left the Creator behind. Following the lead of their founder, Cain, they drew great strength from the works of their hands, but refused to acknowledge their dependence upon the God who gave them the ability to build and create and invent. It was a city marked by loose morals and violence, including well-known instances of murder (Genesis 4:23) and polygamy (Genesis 4:19).

Nowhere in the history of Cain's family, the world's first city-builders, is the mention of God or worship of God. No erecting of altars, any mention of prayer, no cathedrals to the Creator. The generation of Cain would be the architects of a world God later saw fit to destroy with a flood.

So Is Progress Bad?

From the very first society to our current progressive age, every time man has advanced, it has progressed without God, suffering the cruel fate of its own paganism. In his book, *The Beginnings,* Dr. Ray Stedman quotes German theologian Helmut Thielicke:

> *The strange thing is that the closer we come the more clearly we see the red thread that runs like a pulsing, bloody artery through the myriad figures of the world. This motherly earth, on which even the greatest of men walked, on which they erected cities and cathedrals and monuments, has drunk the blood of Abel. And this blood of the murdered and abused appears in stains and rivulets everywhere, including the greatest figures. Cain, the "great brother" and progenitor of mankind,*

*betrays his mysterious presence. Somewhere in
every symphony the tone-figure of death is trace-
able. Somewhere on every Doric column this
mark is to be found. And in every tragedy the
lament over injustice and violence rings out.*

So, you're asking me, does this mean that advancement,
progress, even the building of cities is sinful? Have the
Amish, with their preoccupation with the rural life and
the abandonment of modernity, been right all along?
Am I, writing this book on my sleek laptop, tuned into
my iPhone, and sipping a caffeine-packed soda, in
rebellion against God?

Dr. Ray Stedman concurring with Thielicke's
analysis, offers:

*We have here all the ingredients of modern life—
travel, music and the arts, the use of metals, the
organized political life, and the domestication of
animals. All of this is admirable and progressive,
and, as we have indicated, ultimately intended for
man. Nothing that fallen man longs after was to
be denied him, as far as God was concerned, but it
was to be when man was ready for it.*

So let's put to rest the notion that Christianity and
progress are incompatible, that faith is marked only by
backward living and communal dwelling. Let's remember that it was the Creator God Himself who endowed
man with unique and special gifts, who designed the
human mind to create.

God isn't even against cities. In fact, the New
Jerusalem promised by God in the New Heaven, is in

fact a city so beautiful it will make the skylines of today's modern cities seem like an abandoned rural outpost by comparison (Revelation 21). Hebrews says that those who died in faith *"look for a city whose builder and maker is God"* (Hebrews 11:10). And if you read the prophet Jeremiah's instructions to the exiles in Babylon, it was to be an active part of building the urban landscape.

In fact, history might argue that biblical values, a large part of the successful foundation of Western civilization, have led to the freedom in which new ideas and progress have been birthed. Read the works of men like Rodney Stark (*Cities of God, The Victory of Reason, One True God*) and Dinesh D'Souza (*What's So Great About Christianity?*).

And today technology is being harnessed by the Church for unprec-edented evangelism. Communication, streaming video, online language tools, and Bible software are just a few of the ways the gospel is being stretched to the four corners of the earth. And if you

MAN FORGETS THE SOURCE OF HIS STRENGTH.

travel through the Middle East and many Third-World countries, you'll see satellite dishes on every rooftop and apartment building. Ministries beam the gospel message in places previously unreached by the church.

So if progress isn't the culprit for man's disconnec-tion with God, why do people in the age of progress seem to leave God behind? Paul describes what happens in Romans 1. He succinctly said that man begins to worship the "creature" more than their "Creator." How ironic, but true. Endowed by prosperity, opportunity, and gifted-ness from God, man forgets the source of his strength and the long slow march toward death.

God's Holy Remnant

Thankfully, the writer of Genesis doesn't conclude with the bleak picture of man's rebellion against his God. God always has a remnant, a called-out people, who refuse to bow to the God of reason.

Adam and Eve gave birth to another son. His name was Seth, which means "substitute." Not only was Seth a substitute for his slain brother, Abel, but his life is also a picture of the future substitute, Jesus, who assumed death on behalf of fallen mankind.

At first glance, the accomplishments of Seth's line pale in comparison to that of Cain. There is no impressive legacy of city-building, invention, and development of the arts. But a little line at the end of Genesis , chapter 4, reveals why this family ultimately saved civilization when God determined to judge the world with a flood. Genesis 4:26 reads: *"At that time, people began to call upon the name of the Lord"* (ESV).

It was a humble rebuke to the pride and godlessness that ruled the day. In this age of progress, people of faith understood that the world wasn't in need of the next great technology, but simple acts of faith.

Prayer Still Matters

Genesis 4 offers remarkable parallels and lessons for today's believers. Nowhere does Scripture tell us to apologize or even abandon the modern marvels of our world. You can be a gadget freak and godly. (Sighs of relief heard on iPhones around the world!)

But we're presented with a choice. We can swim in the current of Cain, awash in the excesses of our age, fool ourselves into thinking we're in control of our words, and abandon faith as the relic of an unenlightened past.

Or we can live like Seth's people. We can be known in the pages of history for our devotion to God in an age of godlessness. We begin by knocking down the idols of technology, recognizing man's achievements for what they are—fruits of a magnificent Creator God and tools to be harnessed for His pleasure.

It is the spirit of Cain that robs us of time with God, that convinces us that we're too busy to pray, too important to set aside time for God's church, and too deserving of the good life to sacrifice our treasure for the kingdom.

It's the spirit of Seth that prioritizes God and recognizes prayer's power, especially in an age of progress.

The Spirit of Cain in the Church

If we're not careful, we can develop a spirit of Cain in the church. We can get so involved in doing things for God that we neglect the more important work of knowing God.

I so often see this of my generation. We're a people focused on making an impact; we're zealous about kingdom building and social justice. These works are an important reflection of faith (just ask James). But works alone should come from the overflow of a heart that yearns for God.

I'm reminded of Jesus' gentle rebuke to Martha in Luke 10. Martha was a devoted follower and regarded Mary's time at Jesus' feet as unimportant and unproductive.

I would characterize my generation as a Martha generation. On more than one occasion I've eliminated soul work as an unproductive use of my time, when I could be ministering, helping, creating. We must heed Jesus' rebuke and set aside our busywork for God and renew our time at His feet.

In fact, renewal of our relationship with God leads to more productivity in our work for God. Interestingly, the most remarkable shipbuilder wasn't a descendant of Cain, but of Seth. Noah, it says, found *"grace in the eyes of the Lord."* Against all odds, he spent 100 years constructing the only man-made edifice that would survive God's wrath, the ark.

But guess what Noah's name means. "Rest." That's right. A man whose soul found rest in God built something more enduring than all the generations of Cain.

In fact, all of God's people were builders. Noah built an ark. Abraham built a nation. Moses built a system of worship. Joshua built an army. David built a nation. Solomon built a temple. The apostles built the church.

And so it is that when we begin with God, when we prioritize our lives, when we relinquish control, God builds in us a legacy far greater than we could develop on our own.

Prayer isn't a waste of time; it's the best use of time. It's the very fuel that inspires a life of impact for God's kingdom.

Questions

- What does Coach Dungy's gospel presentation before a Super Bowl audience say about the priorities in his life? In what small ways can average Christians model this kind of God-centric life?
- What did Cain's offer say about his motivations and heart? How does the spirit of Cain rule our society? Our churches? Our homes?
- In what ways do our modern cities resemble the civilizations built by Cain?
- Explain the fallout of man's progress without God.
- Progress and faith have had an uneasy relationship. Does this mean God is against societal progress and innovation?
- In what areas have you allowed busyness to crowd out your walk with God? In what ways can you adjust?

Resources

- I'm always hesitant to recommend books on prayer, not because they aren't good, but because they are, and often their depth is both intimidating and frightening. I suggest you just begin to pray and make prayer a daily priority. Even if you grab 15 minutes in the morning. In the next chapter, we'll explore a more conversational, running dialogue with God.
- This is the approach I've taken in my devotional life. I'm very busy, and I'm prone to Cain-like tendencies toward upward mobility, all at the expense of time with God. So every year my wife and I together buy a good devotional book and go through it together. I try to see if it is available by email, so I can read it on my phone. This daily exercise always refreshes me

and brings me back to square one. It is a great supplement to my weekly study in the Scriptures for prayer. You might try Crosswalk.com and subscribe to one of their email devotionals, such as *My Utmost for His Highest* or some of their more contemporary ones.

Bible

- Genesis 3
- Romans 5
- James 1

when God is offline
How to Pray When the Lights Go Out

Behold, I go forward, but he is not there, and backward, but I do not perceive him; on the left hand when he is working,
I do not behold him; he turns to the right hand, but I do not see him.
—Job 23:8–9 (ESV)

"When darkness veils His lovely face, I rest on His unchanging grace;
In every high and stormy gale, My anchor holds within the veil."
—"The Solid Rock"

Instant messaging (IM-ing) is now one of the most popular ways to communicate. Some people predict it may one day render email obsolete. As a self-admitted fan of Google Talk, I enjoy looking in the left-hand corner and knowing who of my hundreds of contacts may be online.

I think IM-ing is reflective of a generation constantly seeking ways to engage in conversation, which is why it can be frustrating when no friends, real or digital, are online. Even worse is when nobody is reachable by email, IM, Facebook, cell phone, or text. When nobody is available to satiate our desperate need for conversation, we are devastated.

When God Is Offline

Here's a question: *What happens when God goes offline?* Sure, God doesn't mess with Google Talk or AOL Instant Messenger or even Microsoft Live. Though we have all experienced key and often critical moments of life where God seems strangely absent.

Scripture assures us that God never sleeps, that He's all-knowing, ever-present, all-powerful. We understand these truths academically and theologically, but what about those dark nights of the soul when God seems silent?

In the Bible, many wrestled with this question. David. Habakkuk. Moses. But perhaps the most anguished cry comes from a man named Job. Most people have heard of Job, even those who rarely read the Bible. In a way, his life is held up as a worst-case scenario. If we think we have problems, look at Job's life and suddenly our problems are miniscule.

To experience just one of the several excruciating trials Job suffered would devastate most people. And yet Job suffered in every area of his life.

Job was the Warren Buffet of the ancient world, amassing large holdings in livestock and agriculture. He was described by the Book of Job as *"the greatest man in the East."*

Job not only had the distinction of being one of the world's wealthiest men, he was also among the most righteous. This was a label applied by God Himself. In the very first statement of the Book of Job, we read, that he *"was blameless and upright, one who feared God and turned away from evil"* (Job 1:1).

Few men, rich or poor, have that kind of spiritual legacy, but Job lived in such a way that both God and man clearly understood the passion of his heart.

Pick up a copy of *People* or click on *TMZ,* and you can find all you need to know about the corrosive influence of wealth and power. There are infinitely more temptations at that level of life than what is available to us ordinary folks. Yet the size of his bank account or the stature of the people who attended his parties didn't move the needle of Job's faith one degree.

Equally impressive is the way Job passed the legacy of faith down through his family. Each year he offered sacrifices to Jehovah on behalf of his children. This wasn't required by God, but it was an extra statement, like Joshua's declaration to the people of Israel, *"As for me and my house, we will serve the Lord"* (Joshua 24:15).

EVERYONE KNEW WHAT WAS MOST IMPORTANT.

In Job's family, everyone knew what was most important. It wasn't accumulating wealth or climbing the social rungs of power and influence. Worship of Jehovah permeated every area of their family life. God told Satan about Job: *"There is nobody like this man on the earth"* (Job 6:8).

Yet despite his exemplary life, Job endured a series of tragedies, each allowed by God to demonstrate Job's faith and display God's ultimate glory.

He lost his entire portfolio of wealth (Job 1:13–17). Losing camels and donkeys and oxen isn't a big deal to a suburban guy like me, but imagine each animal as a stock in an investment portfolio or the value of your real estate. In one day, Job forfeited his entire net worth. He went from the penthouse to the outhouse, from Fortune 500 to bankruptcy court.

He lost his children (Job 1:18–19). In one horrific accident, Job lost all his children. This is when Job's grief really began. You can lose your net worth. You can lose your job. You can lose your house. But when you lose your kids, you feel you've lost everything. There is no worse tragedy in the human experience.

Job lost his health (Job 2:7–8). As if a crashing portfolio and the loss of his children wasn't enough, Job endured a debilitating health crisis. The Bible says Job was struck with *"loathsome boils"* from head to toe. Scholars are unsure of the exact nature of his illness. Some feel this may have been a combination of leprosy and elephantiasis, a horrific condition that causes the internal organs to bloat and produces a burning, itching sensation in the skin. Whatever it was, Job's condition was so severe it caused his best friends to weep when they first laid eyes on him. His own wife counseled him to *"curse God and die"* (Job 2:9).

Job lost his reputation (Job 4:7–11). As if losing your wealth, your family, and your health wasn't enough, Job saw his once-spotless character attacked. His trials were so severe, they caused Job's closest friends to wonder if

God was trying to send a message. What was Job hiding that lit the fuse of God's wrath?

A Dark Night of the Soul

When we read the story of Job, we're privileged to see behind the curtain of heaven and witness God's purpose in Job's pain. But Job didn't have that backstage pass. All he knew was life got really hard, and God seemed strangely absent. Listen to his aching words:

> *"Behold, I go forward, but he is not there, and backward, but I do not perceive him; on the left hand when he is working, I do not behold him; he turns to the right hand, but I do not see him."*
> —Job 23:8–9 (ESV)

In other words, God was offline. Off the grid. Under the radar. Interestingly, Job's honest pleas are in line with other great men of faith.

- David wondered, "*Why, O Lord, do you stand far away? Why do you hide yourself in times of trouble?*" (Psalm 10:1 ESV).
- Isaiah declared, "*Truly, you are a God who hides himself, O God of Israel, the Savior*" (Isaiah 45:15 ESV).
- *Jesus, on the Cross, cried out, "My God, My God, why have you forsaken Me?"* (Matthew 27:46 ESV).

What are we to do when God is offline? Job gives us some guidance. Misunderstood by family and friends, forced to scrape his badly damaged skin with a potsherd, poverty-stricken, and homeless, he still found hope. He says: *But he knows the way that I take; when he has tried me, I shall come out as gold* (Job 23:10 ESV).

I've seen this passage plastered on calendars and mugs, greeting cards, and bookmarks. But I've never connected it with the previous verse. Put them together and in essence Job says, "In every single situation, God seems to be absent. I cannot see His face. But, I take comfort in knowing that God sees me." *Job couldn't see God, but God could see Job.* That's all he needed to hang on to his faith (Job 23:11).

Job hung the insecurity of his present situation on the security of God's absolute sovereignty. He traded in his feelings for the integrity of God's character. This was the truth that set Job free.

To respond as Job did requires great faith, to be sure. And I understand how tragedy can push someone away from God. Many today turn to atheism as a salve. How could a loving God allow such pain? But in that place without a God, is there any hope?

Maybe I'm a little biased, because I've always known God, from the time I could understand spiritual things. I grew up in a culture of faith. But even a lifelong believer encounters reality that rocks his world. And yet, in times of doubt, when the walls are closing in on me, the knowledge that Someone somewhere understands what's going on gives me the strength to soldier on. I may not like what God is doing, but at least I know He's there and He's got a plan.

This is where Job was. He definitely had issues with God. He didn't much like life in its present condition. He couldn't really see God, but He knew that God could see him. That's all he needed to take his next breath.

Someone once said, "God's hand is invisible but He has an all-seeing eye."

The Furnace of Affliction

Job compared his affliction to a smelting furnace with God as the craftsman. He was sure that after emerging from the fire, he would "come forth as gold."

Trials do have a way of smelting off the dross. The faith that emerges from the furnace is always purer. Would we even know Job, would his story merit biblical consideration if there was not the epic story of his faith on trial? Consider how many lives have been inspired by Job throughout history.

In his letter to the early church, the Apostle James wrote:

> *Behold, we consider those blessed who remained steadfast. You have heard of the steadfastness of Job, and you have seen the purpose of the Lord, how the Lord is compassionate and merciful.*
> —James 5:11 (ESV)

James points to Job as an example not only of enduring faith, but of God's character. Because He's bound by compassion and mercy, He only allows trials that serve to strengthen our character, that work our lives around to reflect the glory of God. Dr. Warren Wiersbe writes, "When God puts His own people into the furnace, He keeps His eye on the clock and His hand on the thermostat. He knows how long and how much. We may question why He does it to begin with, or why He doesn't turn down the heat or even turn it off; but our questions are only evidences of unbelief."

Gold Nuggets in the Darkness

I've seen the gold God produces in the furnace of affliction in the lives of those I serve as pastor. I'm privileged to serve a predominantly older congregation. It's such a treasure to know and learn from men and woman who have lived the years of hardship and have emerged wiser, stronger, and full of confident faith.

Once a month I have breakfast with one of our elders. Jim, a charter member of the Greatest Generation, found Christ on the deck of an aircraft carrier. He met his wife just after the tumult of World War II, and used his hands to build homes and businesses as a carpenter in the Chicagoland area. He's the kind of rugged, faithful laymen who forms the foundation of many of God's churches around the world.

Jim's age has forced him to slow down from his active working days, but his mind is as fertile and rich as any person I've known. When Jim speaks, I shut up and listen because His life has been marked by hardship, his character forged in the fires of God's furnace. He's a rich man for his trials, and I'm privileged to share in those riches.

When I see Jim, I see Job. I imagine Job became a font of wisdom for the generations who sat at his knee and learned of an enduring faith in Jehovah. A faith that perseveres through the worst the enemy can offer.

Why does God go offline? Why does He hide His face? Why does God seem absent from our struggles? I believe the life Job offers four powerful reasons:

1. God hides His face so we will seek Him. Job was a righteous man who honored God in all of his doings. But I wonder if he *craved* God like he did when he lost it all—when it seemed as if God was missing from his life.

We can grow so familiar with God, or at least God-stuff, that our intimacy can wane. But when God veils His face, it causes us to search after Him like a deer after water (Psalm 42:1). God wants to be sought and promises that we'll find Him (Jeremiah 29:13).

2. God hides His face so we will value Him. John Piper has famously said, "God is most glorified in us when we are most delighted in Him." Everything of value was stripped away from Job and yet Job could still say, *"Naked I came from my mother's womb and naked I'll return"* (Job 1:21). Where do we find value? In our accomplishments? In our vocation? In our validation as a man or woman of God? God's desire is for us to find ultimate value in Him.

3. God hides His face to get us to think like Him. Job begged and pleaded with God to reveal Himself, and God eventually answered in one of the most profound passages in the entire Bible. Entire volumes have and could still be written on the weighty theology of Job 38–39. This is where God compares His worldview with Job's and finds that Job's perspective is seriously lacking. God describes in vivid detail His creative genius in speaking the worlds into existence. Essentially His answer to Job's queries is simple. I'm God and you're not.

Job may have felt God's presence missing, but God reminded him that everything he saw, from the rising to the setting of the sun, revealed the glory and the presence of God. Psalm 46:10 says to *"be still and know that I am God."* Not be still and *feel* He is God. God's omniscience, omnipotence, and omnipresence are facts that never change, regardless of our circumstances.

4. ***God hides Himself because we can't handle Him.*** If God revealed all of Himself, we couldn't handle Him. We're touched by the fall, weakened by sin, subject to the limits of humanity. We must trust that there is much more going on than what we see in front of us. Paul says we see through a glass darkly (1 Corinthians 13:12). We only see what we see. But God is so much bigger.

Job's situation was more than just one guy suffering. His problems really weren't with people and property and poor health. There was a cosmic argument taking place in the heavens. And so it is that our trials are not merely unfortunate circumstances. They are major-league tests to see if our faith is real. Ephesians tells us that we battle not against flesh and blood, but against principalities and powers (Ephesians 6:12).

Your troubled marriage is not only about you and your spouse. Your crippling medical condition is not only about one person suffering the cruel fate of an out-of-control, unjust world. Your nightmare at home, the nightmare nobody understands, is more than just another sad story.

There is an unseen world watching, waiting. Will you curse God and die as everyone suggests or will you prove Satan wrong and say with Job, *"Though He slay me, yet I will trust Him"* (Job 13:15).

Questions

- What explains our need for communication and conversation? And how do we reconcile that with a God who sometimes hides?
- Why does God hide His face?
- Can you explain some situations in your life where God seemed emotionally distant?
- How does Job's response to God's seeming absence bring hope?

Resources

- My good friend Cecil Murphey has written a powerful book, *When God Turns Out the Lights*. He writes candidly about his own struggles when God was absent and what he discovered in that journey through the darkness.
- Jerry Sittser has written a number of excellent books on suffering and loss, among them *A Grace Disguised*, *When God Doesn't Answer Your Prayers*
- I would also encourage you to read the Book of Job. But get ready, because God may take you through trials in order to internalize it in your life.

Bible

- Psalm 10
- James 5
- Isaiah 45
- Matthew 27

your divine hotspot
Staying Connected in a Disconnected World

I am the vine; you are the branches. Whoever abides in me and I in him, he it is that bears much fruit, for apart from me you can do nothing.
—John 15:5 (ESV)

"There is only one relationship that matters, and that is your personal relationship to a personal Redeemer and Lord. Let everything else go, but maintain that at all costs, and God will fulfill His purpose through your life.... Always remain alert to the fact that where one man has gone back is exactly where anyone may go back...Kept by the power of God—this is the only safety."
—Oswald Chambers

Two words explain why Panera Bread has become my second office—free Wi-Fi.

And no, I'm not one of those freeloaders who park all day without purchasing any of Panera's delicious products. I've moved up several pants sizes on their cinnamon bagels alone and the hazelnut coffee has sustained many sermons and manuscripts.

Besides delicious food, Panera offers its customers something more: a connection to the outside world. For authors, pastors, businesspeople, and others who rely on the Internet for their livelihood, this is a valuable service.

I'm finding that there are fewer and fewer places *not* connected to the World Wide Web. I have an iPhone and I can go virtually anywhere and check email, find out how badly the Cubs are losing, and update Facebook.

Last year our family drove to the Carolinas for vacation and along the way we spent three days in the beautiful mountains of Asheville, North Carolina. Of course I felt the urgent need to check my email, but apparently 3G hadn't quite climbed the peaks of the Blue Ridge Mountains. (Verizon customers, please don't write me. I see your commercials. I know about your maps.)

Here I was, standing on top of the toilet in our cabin, raising my iPhone to the sky, desperate for a signal. My wife thinks that is pathetic, and she's probably right. But it is an exaggerated symbol of our generation's desperate longing to be connected.

All you have to do is look at a social networking site like Facebook. Five years ago, it was part-time project of a few bored Harvard students. Now it rivals Google as the most visited place on the Internet. Even digitally challenged people from previous generations are all over Facebook, using it to connect to long-lost relatives, forgotten friends, and members of their various community groups.

The promise of the digital age is that anyone can be anywhere and stay connected to the flow of humanity.

You can be in a cab in Boston, a farmhouse in Arkansas, a medical tent in a Third-World disaster zone. With the swipe of a finger, the click of a mouse, or the tapping of keys you are engaged in the ongoing worldwide conversation.

For those of us who have grown up on the grid of technology, we *expect* to be connected. So when we lose that—when the cable is unplugged, the battery dies, or the network fails—we don't know what to do. How many of us could function for a week without access to the Internet? How about a day?

WE EXPECT TO BE CONNECTED.

We'd be lost, because our friendships, our finances, our futures, our meaningful pursuits, our ministries are increasingly dependent connection to the worldwide community.

Jesus and Connection

Enter Jesus. Of course He entered the world long before Facebook or 4G, but His words speak loudly to our generation.

Jesus called His followers to a special kind of connection. In a final discourse before going to the Cross, comparing their relationship to Him to a vine and its branches. Jesus often found natural, normal pieces of daily life to illustrate new spiritual truth. It's possibly Jesus shared this talk as He and the disciples walked from the Upper Room to the Garden of Gethsemane. I've traveled that same pathway and noticed the vines that still blanket the trestles and ancient city walls.

You can almost picture Him reaching over, plucking a branch, and turning toward them, *"I am the vine, you are the branches"* (John 15).

Jesus' words built upon a common metaphor. The prophets of long ago often raised the vine in describing God's people, Israel (Isaiah 5; Jeremiah 2). The vine was a national symbol of freedom from Egypt, minted on every coin. Even the secular King Herod understood the vine's symbolism, encrusting the gates of his new temple with a large gold grapevine.

Jesus' words were given to comfort those who had left everything to follow Him. Each had abandoned full-time occupations to follow this rabbi from Nazareth on the shaky dream that this Christ might bring about the change in society and government for which the Jewish people longed. For three years, they traveled the breadth of the country, spending every moment by the Master's side. With their own eyes they saw Jesus heal the sick, raise the dead, calm the storm, feed the hungry, rebuke the religious, hang out with prostitutes and tax cheats. Along the way, Jesus revealed powerful truths about who He was and what His kingdom will look like.

They had come to believe that Jesus was no ordinary rabbi, but the promised Messiah, the fulfillment of Israel's long-held expectations. The Son of God. Immanuel. God with us.

But God with them didn't mean for the disciples what they thought it would. They didn't understand why the Messiah must first suffer and die as a Lamb slain for sin before He could rule as a conquering King.

Like most Christ followers today, the disciples could only see what was in front of them. They looked for the King to overthrow Rome, a scenario that would put each of them in a place of power and position and influence.

That's why Jesus' final words to His disciples, recorded in detail by John, may be His most important words. Not only do they contain future reality for the disciples, they are words which *directly* apply to us today, who as spiritual descendants of the disciples, live in the heart of the church age.

In the moment, Jesus' words were a bitter pill. He shattered their dreams of political and moral revolution. He would allow Himself to be arrested, tried illegally, and brutally murdered by the religious and political leaders. It would be the highest demonstration of supernatural, *agape* love. Indeed, He laid down His life for His friends (John 15:13).

@

JESUS' FINAL WORDS DIRECTLY APPLY TO US TODAY.

Imagine how this played out in their minds. Their master would be arrested? Would they be strong like they claimed? Would they fight? No, Jesus predicted, they wouldn't. As the prophets foretold, they would scatter like sheep. One would betray Jesus. Another would deny Him.

But this was part of God's plan conceived in the Garden, promised to Adam and Eve, sustained through the chosen people Israel, and carried to fruition by the God-man, Jesus Christ. And death would not be the end.

After three days in a rich man's tomb, Jesus would rise from the dead and in 40 days, He would ascend to heaven.

We can't overestimate how difficult this must have been for them. Their best friend, their leader, their master—He would soon be gone. How would they go on with a Jesus-sized void in their hearts?

We have to assume that Jesus was experiencing His own set of mixed emotions. Sure, as God, it was His joy to fulfill the will of the Father, set down in eternity. But as a human, He'd miss those close moments He spent with His closest friends. I'm guessing the tears flowed freely in the Upper Room, even among the rugged men of Palestine.

Yet Jesus knew their thoughts. And in the midst of His final address, He reassured them with a powerful promise.

He would leave the disciples, but the disciples wouldn't be left alone. In fact, Jesus said that their lives *after* His departure from the earth would be more powerful and more effective than the three and a half years they spent with Jesus at their side (John 14:2).

What could be better than God in the flesh, the *logos* living alongside them? How about God *in* them?

> *I will ask the Father, and he will give you another Helper, to be with you forever* (John 14:16 ESV).

God was leaving, but God was returning. The Son would ascend so the Spirit could descend.

The presence of the Holy Spirit was something about which the patriarchs and prophets of the past could dream. In the Old Testament, the Holy Spirit would *come upon*, *enable* and *be with* God's people, but Jesus prophesied of a new and different age, when the

Holy Spirit would permanently *indwell* all who believed in Christ.

This was better than Jesus *among* them or Jesus *alongside* them. Better than God's power manifested in nature or in clouds or fires or bushes. Jesus was leaving precisely so they could experience the fullness of God's power *in* them.

The outpouring of the Spirit would launch a new age of the church (Acts 2) and become a reality for *every* believer who has since put their faith in the risen Christ (1 Corinthians 12:13; Romans 8:9; Ephesians 1:13–14).

That's why you open the Book of Acts and find a new and different set of men than those you read about in the Gospel accounts. These same disciples laid the foundation of Christ's church, boldly preaching the gospel to the nations, enduring persecution, and willingly giving their lives in martyrdom for their Lord.

Today, the church extends into every corner of the globe, serving as the hands and feet of Jesus, proclaiming the radical message of salvation by faith in Christ alone.

This is the mystery and beauty and power of God in us.

Power Outage in the Promised Land

Abide in me and I in you (John 15:4 ESV).

In the nearly 2,000 years since those words left the lips of Jesus, His followers have wrestled with the full implications of God in us. Today, theologians wrestle, denominations fight, and the average believer barely understands what it means to fully experience the wonder and power of the Holy Spirit.

What we do know is that Jesus didn't offer another religious system or another lifestyle. To a people weary of legalistic burdens, Jesus offered what the human soul most craves: intimacy with God. Jesus' death, burial, and resurrection provided the conduit for the Creator to have fellowship once again with the crown of His creation.

Jesus offered an *abiding* relationship with God, enabled by the Son, through the indwelling Holy Spirit. To *abide* means to stay, to linger, to dwell. What the disciples experienced in their three years of ministry was special, but it was a series of personal encounters. But what Jesus offered through the Holy Spirit was a permanent, lifelong connection. God would come to stay.

Even though the disciples didn't completely understand what Jesus was saying, I imagine these words were a balm to their soul.

Jesus would ascend, but God's Spirit would descend. God was leaving yet lingering. He was dying, yet He would dwell in them.

This is an invitation still open to Jesus' followers. And yet, I must admit that as a lifelong Christian, I wonder what I've done with the reality of God in me. I've been around Jesus—church, prayer, the Bible, Christian books—for almost 30 years and yet, do I really know what it is to linger with Him?

Like most Christians, I've often viewed spirituality as a way to refuel, like a thirsty gas tank after a day on the interstate. Go to church, get fired up, and hope it lasts until at least Tuesday. Maybe during the week you have the courage to open your Bible and read and pray. You might get doses of the Spirit while listening to a sermon or a favorite worship song.

But lingering? Abiding? It seems Jesus intended abiding to be more than a stop-and-go spiritual recharge.

Perhaps a real-world, twenty-first-century illustration will explain.

A few years ago, I traveled to India with a mission team. We stayed on the outskirts of a small town at a mission compound. While I thoroughly enjoyed my visit, I could never get used to the substandard electric supply. It was so unreliable that the compound required the use of generators 24 hours a day.

It was hard to accomplish anything of significance, at least electronically. Many times a day the power would go out, forcing the firing of the generator. It constantly flickered on and off. So typical tasks like charging a cell phone, setting an alarm clock, even sending an email were an adventure.

For the Indian pastors and missionaries, this was their life, so it rarely bothered them. But for us Americans, it was maddening. We wondered, *Can we do anything? Can we fix the power supply? This can't continue.*

If this happened even for a day or two in the States, we'd be on the phone to the electric company demanding a fix.

This is a earthy example of how Christians often approach God's presence in our lives. Like the missionaries, we have gotten too used to intermittent bursts of power, content to wait for the periodic recharges of church and prayer and devotional life. We cross in and out of spiritual activity, living from high-to-high with a lot of powerless living in between.

We may get daily recharges time in the Word or a weekly experience at church. We may get a super power boost from a Christian concert or Bible conference. But in the day-to-day meat grinder of life, we often live disconnected from God and are therefore indistinguishable from those who don't know God and therefore don't have the availability of the Holy Spirit's presence.

What would happen if we approached spiritual power outages with the same urgency as a real electricity failure? How would our families, our churches, our communities change? Maybe this is why so many of us live frustrated, unfulfilled, often sinful Christian lives.

Jesus invites us to linger, because, in His words, *"Without me, you can do nothing"* (John 15:5). Does that mean we can accomplish nothing at all on the strength of our human talents and abilities? No, we can actually accomplish a great deal. But when we live and work and perform without His power, we lack the real fruit of a sanctified, set-apart life. Fruit that is often hard to find in the church, such as love, joy, peace, gentleness, goodness, faith (Galatians 5:22–23).

@

WE OFTEN LIVE DISCONNECTED FROM GOD.

In reality, our Christian experience all too often resembles the appliance hooked up to that unstable, intermittent Indian power supply. Sure, the lights come on and it may even function well in short bursts. But ask that appliance to do or create anything of lasting significance and you're asking for the impossible.

Step into the River

Besides His use of the vine, Jesus used another simple metaphor to describe the work of the Spirit. Water.

Every year at the Feast of Tabernacles, water was poured over the head of the high priest, symbolizing the flow of God's grace. One year, at the height of this ceremony, Jesus stood and said, *"If any man thirst, let him come unto me, and drink. He that believeth on me, as the scripture hath said, out of his belly shall flow rivers of living water"* (John 7:38–39).

Jesus spoke of flowing water, rushing rivers, words that resonate in a climate where water was a premium. I've traveled through the hot Middle Eastern desert and saw for myself the value of a rushing, flowing stream. It is life to those who thirst.

And the people of His day were spiritually dry. They participated in outward religious exercises, but down deep they had no connection to God. They were empty.

Jesus offered the same promise to the woman at the well whose pursuit of love also left her wanting. If she drank of Him, Jesus said, she'd not only be satisfied, but she'd be transformed into a *"well of water springing up into eternal life"* (John 4:14).

Jesus offers that same flow of living water to you and to me today. To know and experience the life of the Holy Spirit shouldn't be abnormal for the believer, *because this is the life we were created for, the life Jesus came to restore and redeem.*

Jesus satisfies the thirsty longing in every soul. David spoke of a river, whose streams *"make glad the city of God"* (Psalm 46:4 KJV). In Revelation, John describes Heaven as having a river that flows from the throne of God, *"Let the one who is thirsty come; let the one who desires take the water of life without price"* Revelation 22:17 (ESV).

The Spirit is a river. That river has life. It has power. It nourishes the soul.

Abiding 101

So how does a believer *abide* with Jesus? What does it look like to step into the river of God's awesome power?

Four-hour prayer sessions before the sun rises?

Marathon Bible studies?

Seventeen pages of journaling?

Now, this book is not a treatise on the work of the Spirit. Better Bible teachers have spoken on the breadth of yielding to the Holy Spirit. I have personally benefited from books like *The Holy Spirit* by Dr. Charles Ryrie and more recently, *Forgotten God* by Francis Chan.

But I'd like to share a few basic principles that apply to this relationship. Keep in mind as we go, that the Holy Spirit is not a system to be applied. He is a Somebody to be worshipped, reverenced, and obeyed.

In his letters to the early church, Paul wrote extensively about the Holy Spirit, unpacking the seedlings of truth delivered to the disciples at the Last Supper. When we add Paul's words to those of Jesus, we get a comprehensive body of truth that helps us in our relationship with this mysterious presence of God in us.

Throughout the New Testament, Paul gives basic action items that clue us in on harnessing the power of the Spirit in our lives, opening the door for genuine transformation.

- **Recognize**
  > In light of what Scripture reveals, you would think that all Christians were aware of the presence of the Holy Spirit living inside them. Yet many are unaware that He is part of their inheritance as a believer. Twice Paul reminded the church:

  >> *Or do you not know that your body is a temple of the Holy Spirit within you, whom you have from God? You are not your own* (1 Corinthians 6:19 ESV).

  >> *Do you not know that you are God's temple and that God's Spirit dwells in you?* (1 Corinthians 3:16 ESV).

  > These words were delivered in the midst of a stinging rebuke to the church at Corinth, whose believers had succumbed to the sexual looseness of their culture. He was reminding them that their bodies were now not their own, but were God's. He indwelt them.

  > Very few evangelism presentations include teaching on the Holy Spirit. Why is that? I'm not sure, but perhaps in our rush to get people saved—a good thing—we exclude precious truths that will help them enjoy their new relationship with God and experience His transforming power.

- **Yield**
  > In Romans 6, Paul shares a candid admission of his own personal struggles against the power of sin. But in the midst of his struggle, he is reminded that sin no longer has to have a stranglehold on his life. He urges believers to *yield* themselves to the power and control of the Holy Spirit:

  >> *Do you not know that if you present yourselves to anyone as obedient slaves, you are slaves of the one whom*

you obey, either of sin, which leads to death, or of obedience, which leads to righteousness? (Romans 6:16 ESV).

> What does it mean to yield? It means to allow the Spirit to take the lead. There is the choice to yield to the impulses of our flesh or to yield to the prompts of the Holy Spirit, who lives inside of us. Elsewhere we are commanded to be *"filled with the Spirit"* (Ephesians 5:18). This doesn't necessarily mean we have more of the Holy Spirit, but that we allow the Holy Spirit to have more of us. It's easy to view the Spirit as a sort of jogging buddy instead of a member of the Godhead. God doesn't follow His Creation. God leads His Creation. Paul told the Romans, *"For all who are led by the Spirit of God are sons of God"* (Romans 8:14 ESV). The call of a believer's life is to die to self, to crucify the flesh, and to submit daily to the Spirit of God.

@

JESUS RESISTED THE URGE OF THE IMMEDIATE.

• **Pray**

> First Thessalonians 5:17, almost the shortest verse in the Bible, encourages us to *"pray without stopping."* I've always read this and thought, *well, God can't possibly expect me to bow the knee 24 hours a day, so I guess I have holy permission to skip it.* I never fully grasped what the Scripture was saying until I linked it with Jesus' words in John 15, which invite us to abide. Paul is echoing Jesus' words, urging an open line of communication with God. Paul envisions for the Thessalonians believers a running dialogue with the Father. Is this possible? Imagine how our everyday lives would change if we kept the line open? I'm picturing a news anchor with an earpiece. Backstage, a producer is constantly

giving instructions, telling the anchor what segment is next, who the next guest will be, which camera to look toward. Imagine life with Jesus in your ear as you're speaking with your boss, while you're arguing with your wife, as you engage in conversation with your neighbor. Both John 15 and 1 Thessalonians 5:17 imply that this is possible because of the presence of the Holy Spirit.

- **Walk**
  - ➤ More than 90 times the New Testament uses the term *walk*. The original Greek word, *peripateite* [peh-rih-pah-TAY-the], means to "keep on walking." It implies a lifestyle, a different way of living than what is considered "normal" by the world. Walking in the Spirit is the only way to live the life God called us to live, to be holy, dedicated, and distinct: *But I say, walk by the Spirit, and you will not gratify the desires of the flesh* (Galatians 5:16 ESV). I encourage you to read the entire chapter of Galatians 5 as well as Romans 6–8. It is a powerful chapter on the two choices that face every believer. We can *walk* in the sinfulness of our flesh or we can *walk* in the power of the Holy Spirit. Now there is no believer on earth who always walks in the power of the Spirit, but as we grow in maturity and faith, we should endeavor to walk more frequently in the Spirit's power. And it's not something that we work. It's letting go and allowing the Spirit to flow through us like the river Jesus promised. It's saying no to ourselves.

- **Don't quench**
  - ➤ Did you know that the Holy Spirit's power can actually be turned on and off? In writing to the Thessalonians, Paul warned them not to *"quench the*

Spirit" (1 Thessalonians 5:19). Elsewhere, Paul urged Timothy to *"fan the flames"* of the Holy Spirit's work in him (2 Timothy 1:6; 4:14). He is drawing on the illustration of the Holy Spirit as a fire. He wants to burn through the lives of God's people, but often we can ignore His leadings and promptings. I believe this happens every single day. I know that in my own life, the Spirit has prompted me to talk to a neighbor about salvation or to write an encouraging note to my wife. At times He's telling me to back away from the computer screen and give one of my kids a hug.

➤ We can also do our part to quench the work of the Spirit in the community of believers in which we serve. How often have we older, smarter, wiser saints cooled the fires of an excited new believer because he might have a new or radical idea for ministry that made us feel uncomfortable? I know I have.

➤ I believe this is the singular problem of many otherwise doctrinally sound churches across America. Theologically, we're as tight as can be, but we are so afraid of making a mistake, so safe and guarded in our approach, we thwart the work of the Spirit. I believe this was one of the purposes of the rebuke the Spirit gave to the church at Ephesus in John's blistering letter, shared in Revelation. He said to them, *"You've lost your first love"* (Revelation 2:4). It is possible for believers to be so safe, to be so stuck in tradition, routine, and comfort that we actually shut off the flow of the Spirit's power. I think the enemy is delighted by Christians like this.

• **Don't grieve**
➤ I've often ignorantly or flippantly referred to the Holy Spirit as an "it," when I should respect and honor

Him as a Person, a member of the Godhead, God in me. Imagine having Jesus by your side 24/7 as the disciples did. Imagine Him at your dinner table, in the locker room, in the cubicle as you interact with your co-workers. I'm guessing you would watch the behavior and would live in a way that invites His pleasure. Actually you don't have to imagine, because God *is* with us always in the presence of the Holy Spirit. And He is grieved when we sin. *Because He is God.*

➤ Truthfully, nowhere does the New Testament tell us explicitly that the Holy Spirit gets angry with us when we sin. We do know that He is grieved when we sin. This tells us all we need to know about the heart of God. God isn't some angry cosmic automaton, who is only there to crush us when we mess up. To be sure, Scripture is clear that God hates sin, but God loves sinners. He weeps with sinners. He desperately longs to bring His people out of the bondage of sin back into an abiding relationship with Him. If we think of the Holy Spirit as a Person, as Jesus sitting alongside us, then when we are faced with temptation, we'll think of how our sin deeply grieves and hurts the Holy Spirit. Imagine causing Jesus to shed tears and weep over a choice we made? Love for God is always, always a better motivator than fear of God.

@

IMAGINE CAUSING JESUS TO SHED TEARS AND WEEP.

● **Put on**

➤ Three separate times, to three separate churches, Paul instructed his readers to "put on" Christ (Romans 13:14; Ephesians 4:24; Colossians 3:10). The original Greek word actually refers to the "stepping into a garment." I imagine Paul envisions the soldier who must step into his uniform every morning. That uniform defines who he is to be that day. There are certain activities and places he cannot go, because he wears the official uniform of the armed forces of his country. Galatians 3:27 says that by virtue of our faith in Christ, we are clothed in Christ. But on a practical level, every single day we make a choice. Some days we choose several times during the day. The choice is simple. Whose desires will we serve? Our own or the Holy Spirit who lives inside of us? What kind of person will we be? Whose uniform will we wear? The clothes of the enemy or the uniform of the Holy Spirit? What if we asked ourselves, before our feet touched the floor, *What presence will I serve today? My flesh or the Holy Spirit who dwells in me?* We really don't have a choice *if* we're going to be clothed, but we do have a choice of *whose clothing* we wear.

Before we end this chapter, I want to stress wholeheartedly that this "list" is not really a list at all. Christians are weary of one more system. But I hope that it helps us to think of our relationship with God in fresh new terms. I hope we ditch the urge to take occasional gulps of God and hope it lasts long enough until the next spiritual refill.

The heart of God is expressed by Jesus, who not only promised to abide with us, to linger, to stay, to make His home in our hearts through the Spirit. It is also expressed by Jesus' invitation to us, to enjoy this intimacy with God, intimacy made possible only because He laid down His life for us, His friends.

Questions

- Our generation has a longing to be connected to the larger human conversation online. What does this say about our God-given desire for community and for relationship?
- Why do you think we often find our connections unfulfilling?
- What is so unique about Jesus' invitation to abide?
- How does your relationship with God differ from what Jesus envisioned at the Last Supper?
- How have you approached the Person of the Holy Spirit? Have you treated Him like a Person or an It?
- What attributes about the Spirit have you learned from our study that may shape your view of God in us?

Resources

- I was thoroughly undone by Francis Chan's powerful book, *Forgotten God*. Chan really doesn't deliver any new information about the Spirit, but he takes what the Bible says, what we all know to be true, and drills down deep into the average Christian life and wonders why it is that we honestly don't live as though the Spirit indwells us. I wholeheartedly encourage you to read this book. I believe Chan is a modern-day A. W. Tozer.
- If you have little or no knowledge of the Holy Spirit, I can't recommend more highly Dr. Charles Ryrie's classic, *The Holy Spirit*. Dr. Ryrie has a way of making classic, important theology readable and understandable.

- I had the privilege of hearing John Ortberg speak live at a pastor's function a few years ago. He was talking from his book, *The Me I Want to Be*. The title sounds like typical, self-serving pop-Christianity. It is anything but that. Ortberg really helps us clear through the Christianese and confusion, and helps Christians walk more closely with the Spirit.

Bible

- John 14–16
- Galatians 5
- 1 Thessalonians 5
- 1 Corinthians 2
- Romans 8
- Ephesians 4

trojan horse
The Virus That Disconnects

If I regard iniquity in my heart, the Lord will not hear me:
—Psalm 66:18 (KJV)

"Sin and the child of God are incompatible. They may occasionally meet; they cannot live together in harmony"
—John R. W. Stott

Several years ago, I received an email from a prominent syndicated newspaper columnist, requesting my opinion. Attached was an article he had drafted. As a beginning writer, I was flattered. I assumed his email was a response to an email I had send a month earlier after reading one of his columns. *He must have thought highly of my email.*

Chest swelling with pride, I opened the attachment, read his short piece, and send it back with a few editorial comments. *What a step in my career,* I thought, *soon other Pulitzer Prize–winning columnists will be knocking on my office door.*

The next day I arrived early at the office. I fired up my computer and scanned my email. There was a new email from this guy in my inbox. I clicked on it and read his reply.

"Huh, what is this?" he asked. He said he didn't know who I was, wasn't asking my advice, and was the victim of a nasty computer virus. Apparently a Trojan horse had hijacked his email address book, sending emails and attachments to people around the world.

And guess what? The same virus was now combing through my address book and sending similar virus-infected appeals for advice.

It was my first introduction to the growing new world of malicious computer software.

Of course I'm much more discerning now. I never open an email attachment or hyperlink unless I'm aware of the person who has sent it. And today's battery of software typically catches most malicious spam.

A Virus of the Faith

The Bible warns of a virus that threatens our communication with God. In Psalm 66 David shares: *"If I regard iniquity in my heart, the Lord will not hear me"* (Psalm 66:18 KJV).

So far we have explored the path to and power of an intimate relationship with God. We've witnessed God's heart in pursuing a relationship with His Creation.

But the time has come for us to discuss the subject Christians rarely enjoy, the effect of unconfessed sin in the heart of a child of God.

I find it interesting that David shares his warning about sin in the context of a beautiful psalm of worship.

Psalm 66 speaks of God's faithfulness to Israel, leading them through the Red Sea, conquering their enemies in battle, and providing manna in wilderness. He challenges God's people, both corporately and individually, to engage in unhindered worship of the LORD, because He is worthy. He shares of his own personal worship, sacrifices which symbolize David's total surrender.

Today, as God works through believers in the church age, our worship looks a bit different. We don't offer burnt offerings. Nobody brings a lamb to church (I hope). Instead, we have Jesus, the spotless Lamb of God, a once-and-for-all sacrifice. Yet, in a sense, we mimic David's gifts, because as true followers of Christ, we're to lay down our bodies on the altar, presenting God with a living sacrifice (Romans 12:2).

I'm struck by the heart of David's worship. He keeps nothing back in describing the depth of his feelings toward the Lord. If anyone were to ask, he would tell them how great the Lord is. Isn't that how we feel in worship? I'm hoping you've experienced times like this, where God speaks so powerfully that you burst forth with joy. If you were to visit my office on a Friday, you'd see me this way. After I've wrapped up my study for Sunday, having been powerfully transformed by the Word, I'm pumped and ready to declare God's awesome power. Check my Facebook or Twitter those days. They are typically filled with snippets of what God has planted in my heart for Sunday.

@

CHECK MY FACEBOOK OR TWITTER THOSE DAYS.

You may have similar moments. Perhaps you're listening to a message on Christian radio or tuned in to one of your favorite worship songs. And the Spirit just uses the moment to speak powerfully into your soul. At that moment you're in full, total surrender.

It is in this holy context that David brings up the one thing that can ground our worship, our intimacy, our connection to God to a screeching halt: unconfessed sin.

If Sin Is Forgiven, How Can It Still Be There?

Many Christians wonder, *If Jesus died and paid for my sin on the Cross, how can sin still be present in my life?* The Apostle John tackled this very issue a straightforward letter to the early church. Written to believers, 1 John warns of the presence of unconfessed sin:

> *This is the message we have heard from him and proclaim to you, that God is light, and in him is no darkness at all. If we say we have fellowship with him while we walk in darkness, we lie and do not practice the truth.*
>
> *But if we walk in the light, as he is in the light, we have fellowship with one another, and the blood of Jesus his Son cleanses us from all sin. If we say we have no sin, we deceive ourselves, and the truth is not in us. If we confess our sins, he is faithful and just to forgive us our sins and to cleanse us from all unrighteousness. If we say we have not sinned, we make him a liar, and his word is not in us.*
> —1 John 1:5–10 (ESV)

Those who have put their faith in the work of Jesus on Calvary have seen their sins forgiven. In the eyes of God, they are as righteous as Jesus Christ (2 Corinthians 5:21). Theologians call this *positional sanctification.* It simply means we have been rescued from the *penalty* of sin. Judicially and legally, we're declared "not guilty."

Yet as believers we still sin every day. It's paid-for sin, but it is sin. And we won't be rid of it until we reach the shores of heaven and our glorification is complete.

Before salvation, we were *enslaved* by sin. After salvation, we *wrestle* with sin. Before salvation, we were *condemned* by sin. After salvation, we have access to the throne of God where we *appropriate His grace* for our sin.

@

Even a Christian as mature as the Apostle Paul admitted his struggles. In Romans 6–8, he candidly reveals his deepest internal battle between a new nature that desires to please God and an old nature that desperately hates the things of God.

A CHRIST FOLLOWER HAS A CHOICE.

This is what 1 John is all about. A Christ follower has a choice. He can walk in the power of the Holy Spirit or he can continue to submit to the carnal desires of his old nature.

A true believer will never lose his status as one of God's children. God's promise of love and eternal life are unconditional and secure (John 10:28; 1 John 5:13; Ephesians 4:30). His future in heaven is secure.

Yet the presence of sin isolates us from fellowship with God. Nobody had a more intimate relationship with God than David did. David was a man aligned with God's own heart. And so David understood what got in the way of his walk with God. It was sin, pure and simple. The King James Bible translates his words, "*If I regard iniquity in my heart, the Lord will not hear me."* Other translations employ the word, *cherish* instead of *regard.* Essentially David is speaking of a lingering over, a pursuit of, a dwelling on, sin.

I'm reminded of the words of the prophet Isaiah:

> *But your iniquities have made a separation between you and your God, and your sins have hidden his face from you so that he does not hear.*
> —Isaiah 59:2 (ESV)

Sin clouds our view of God, forming a wall of separation, so that even if we are one of His children, we don't *feel* connected. This is why many who fall away from the Lord question their identity. *Am I really a Christian?* they wonder.

This isn't necessarily because they aren't truly saved, but because their sin has created a barrier in their relationship with God.

Perfect People Preferred?

So if the reality is that we sin every day and if sin keeps us from the heart of God, does that mean nobody really can experience the intimacy Jesus promised to His disciples in John 15? What's the point? Does God only hear the prayer of perfect people?

If that were the case, every one of us would be disqualified and God would have to dismiss all the heroes of Scripture. Hebrews 11 would have to be edited out of Scripture.

So what do the words of David and Isaiah mean?

The key is in the phrase, *"If I regard iniquity"* (KJV). The English Standard Version says, *"If I cherish sin."*

It isn't so much the *fact* of sin that hurts our fellowship, but a heart of willful, persistent sin. An unwillingness to confess known sin and seek repentance and victory through the Holy Spirit.

For instance, picture someone battling with a tough addiction. Does he have to wait until he has completely mastered that addiction before he can pray? No, actually the Holy Spirit can empower him to gradually overcome that sin by yielding more of himself to the Spirit.

This is where the Holy Spirit enters the picture. It is His job to bring to light our sin. It is our job to confess it and immediately allow Him to restore the flow of divine grace into our lives (1 John 1:9).

Confession must be a regular part of a believer's daily walk. It should be as regular as breathing. It's how we keep "short accounts" with God—through the power of the Holy Spirit.

When we reject the Spirit's leading in exposing our sin, two things happen. We quench the divine flow of power from God (1 Thessalonians 5:19) and we grieve the Spirit (Ephesians 4:30.) We remember from our study of the Spirit in chapter 8 that the Spirit is not some force or an "it" but a Person, a member of the Trinity. He is God.

When we ignore our sin, we grieve the heart of God and we cut off ourselves from His divine power.

Naked Before God

But we don't really like to talk about sin. When sin is exposed, our natural reaction has always been the same. We see this brilliantly demonstrated in the Garden, when Adam and Eve were confronted by God. They covered (Genesis 3:7); they hid (Genesis 3:8); they blamed (Genesis 3:12–13). Naked before God, exposed as sinners, they were shamed. And yet, we see in God's response to the sin of our First Family the hope found in transparency.

The knowledge of their sin brought the promise of restoration and hope through the future sacrifice of a Redeemer. Today, we're on the other side of the Cross. The nakedness and shame of our sin is what first brought us to Calvary. And it's the same transparency that will ultimately open up the floodgates of God's restorative grace.

The truth is that an omniscient God doesn't need us to make Him aware of our sin. Hebrews 4:13 reminds us that "all things are naked and open" to God. So God isn't in heaven depending on our ability to self-report our sin. He already is aware of it and He has already received the payment for it, thanks to Jesus' sacrifice on our behalf.

But God is interested in making *us* aware of our sin. For our hearts to be naked and open to us. That transparency and authenticity invites the Spirit to sanctify us and bring our thinking more in line with His.

So confession of sins is more about us agreeing with God's already formed assessment of our condition. Because as long as we invite sin, welcome sin, hide sin, cover sin, we're disagreeing with God and in our disagreement, we can't enjoy intimacy. Amos 3:3 asks, *"Can two walk together, unless they are agreed?"*

Room for One

The Scriptures speak of the jealousy of God (Exodus 34:14). He created us with a free will and desperately desires that we pursue Him exclusively. He designed our hearts with room for one only. No person, Jesus said, can serve two masters. *"Either he will hate the one and love the other, or he will be devoted to the one and despise the other."*

Sin is against the very character of a holy and righteous God. God cannot abide with darkness. So the Christian is continually faced with a choice of which way he will choose, whose allegiance will occupy her heart. Will we grieve God by embracing sin or will we love God by admitting, confessing, and repenting of sin?

@

I'M AFRAID OUR GENERATION OF BELIEVERS TREATS SIN AS A PASSING NUISANCE.

God also demands an authentic lifestyle, not only because of His desire to be glorified and loved exclusively, but because He knows the destructive power of continuing sin in our lives.

In the Garden, Satan presented sin as beautiful, easy, and full of pleasure (Genesis 3), but he is a liar (John 8:44). The truth is that sin always leads to death (James 1:15). Not just physical death, but death of our intimacy with God. Death to our deepest human relationships. Death to our reputations.

I'm afraid our generation of believers treats sin lightly, as if it is a passing nuisance. Perhaps that's why we don't experience the full power of the Spirit. We've covered up, excused, and justified sin as mistakes, failures, preferences. Like the Corinthian church, we're proud of our tolerance, as if we've reached an enlightened state of living that sin no longer affects us.

I'm not normally a doomsday guy, but it doesn't take a rocket scientist to see that sin has been treated lightly in today's evangelical church. Most surveys conclude that rates of divorce, pornography, materialism, and unfaithfulness are as much a problem among God's people as they are in the world.

I believe the church needs revival. Not political revival where everyone agrees with our views on tax cuts, immigration policy, and health care, but revival that is first *personal*, a work of the Spirit among the people of God. We need conviction and awareness of sin, a holy hunger for more of God and less of selfishness.

What Confession Doesn't Mean

I have to be honest. I truly wrestled with a chapter on sin, because I have seen this biblically important topic twisted and used as a cudgel for legalism. When you write a chapter or preach a sermon on sin, what inevitably happens is that some well-meaning, but misguided believers interpret the Bible's clear teaching on confession and repentance as a call to more rules, more outward conformity, and more of what Jesus really hates: man-made religion.

So I want to balance out what we've discussed about sin with some important biblical truths:

First, God doesn't need any more Pharisees. I used to think that unless someone adopted the exact same standards as me, especially in the gray areas, they would be "out of God's will." God has graciously shown me that this was a severe case of pride on my part. The truth is that while there are many clear-cut, concrete commands, there are also plenty of issues which God has deliberately *not spoken or made clear*. For me to add my opinion is extrabiblical.

I may have a personal conviction about an issue, and if God has brought that to my attention, I should obey the Spirit in that area. But I'm in sin if I point the finger in judgment at someone else who doesn't see it that way. This is legalism, and to justify our pride, we render judgments on them like, "God won't bless them because they don't _____." The truth is that they may have a purer heart than I do. For a biblical treatment of this, I recommend Paul's detailed exposition on "meat offered to idols" in 1 Corinthians 8.

The bottom line is that God isn't looking for more Pharisees who make the outside clean (Luke 11:39). God is in search of authentic, humble believers, who pursue obedience and truth in an intimate relationship with Him. His desire is for us to take the magnifying glass off of our brothers and sisters in the pew next to us and to ask the Holy Spirit to apply it to us.

Second, God isn't waiting for you to be perfect to work through you. Everyone one of us struggle with what the Bible refers to as a *"besetting sin"* (Hebrews 12:1). For some, it's a neatly hidden struggle with worry or fear or gossip. For others, it's a visible battle with an addiction.

Does this mean you're not useful to God until you completely overcome your besetting sin? No. In fact, the only way you overcome your sin is through the power of the Spirit working through you.

What confession means is that you are sensitive to the Spirit and when you do sin, you immediately confess it and seek God's restoration. It's about the direction of your heart.

Third, life with God is not about adherence to a list of rules. Legalism provides an easy trap. Give me the list of ten things I'm not supposed to do. If I can check those off, I must be fine. The problem is that the list changes from church to church. Even people within a particular church debate the nonessentials. Some families consider certain entertainment choices as taboo. Others enjoy them with abandon.

Spirituality measured by a list is easier, because we can visually see who is "on God's team" and who isn't. But that is man-centered, humanistic thinking. First Samuel 16:7 says that it is man who looks at outward appearances, but God who looks at the heart.

Genuine spiritual maturity involves transformation of the heart instead of simplistic conformity (Romans 12:2). The earmarks of a connected Christian are the spiritual forms of fruit mentioned in Galatians 5:22–23, not the ever-changing standards of the list-lovers.

Who, Me?

I'm struck by the fire in John's words, written to a second- and third-generation church that had grown immune to their own sin. We typically pluck out 1 John 1:9, the "confession verse" and ignore the two verses that bookend it.

First John 1:8 says, "*If you think you don't have sin, you're deceiving yourself.*" We typically use this verse as a proof text for the presence of sin in a believer's life. But I think John's purpose is more personal.

No Christian can claim to be sinless, at least none that I know. "Of course," we say, "I'm a sinner. Everyone's a sinner." Yet that can be a cop-out. The "nobody's perfect" defense.

I think John is dialing down and asking us to

consider specific situations. We tend to avoid this self-examination. When the preacher shares a sermon on gossip, we immediately think of our family members, our neighbors, our friends who fail to control their tongues. When a conflict arises in the church, the sin can't possibly be on our part. It is always the other guy. When we're confronted by a mature believer about questionable choices, typically we are ready with a list of reasons why we're right.

John says that when we live this way, when we resist the searchlight of the Holy Spirit, we live in a world of self-deception, where we are always right. We make our own rules and nobody can ever approach us about needed change.

This is where God gets personal. It's up to us to keep our walk with Christ strong by choosing the authentic life that is open and reflective, in every situation, to the possibility of sin.

I'm humbled by Paul's authenticity. He declared himself *"the chief of sinners"* (1 Timothy 1:15). How would our relationships change, if in every situation, every conflict, we said, "I am the chief of sinners." What if we abandoned our inclination to defend ourselves and to always be right and allowed for the possibility that, yes, it may be we who are in the wrong?

That doesn't mean we walk around with a sort of martyr, poor-me, doormat-Christian mentality. It doesn't mean we always say "sorry" when it's not warranted. I don't think Paul or John carried themselves like this. If our character is under attack, we have a right to defend it. Yet, even in the times when we are 100 percent right, what if we acted with humility and realized that growth is needed?

What would happen is that we'd open the door for amazing spiritual transformation. Imagine how our families, our churches, our organizations would look if there was a culture of self-reflection and self-examination?

The refusal to acknowledge our own sin not only puts us in a world of self-denial, but it also sets us against God. In 1 John 1:10, John says that when we refuse to accept the reality of our sin, we call God a liar.

I have seen this in living color: Christians who live in their own world, with their own set of rules and their own code of right and wrong. In many ways, the world John describes is legalism. It's a human-directed holiness. And I've noticed that when you offer to bring the Bible to the table, there is a defensiveness and anger.

Authentic living is different. It is the willingness to live naked before God, to allow every situation to be a learning, teaching, growing experience. Authentic believers don't make up their own rules of living. They are slavish to the Word of God as their guide and nothing else.

This is why I believe God calls us to live out our faith in community, to be accountable to a local body of believers, who live their lives around the Word of God. Many today are tempted to live as Lone-Ranger, independent Christians. Burned out by negative church experiences, many in our generation are turning to other forms of community and worship.

But our own vulnerability to the virus of sin that lurks in the heart is the very reason we must take our calling as believers seriously. If we truly desire to walk in intimacy with our Savior, we'll get serious about living apart from sin.

Questions

- A believer has been redeemed from the power of sin and the penalty of sin, but why does he still face the battle with sin in his or her daily life?
- Why is sin so corrosive to our relationship with God?
- What are some ways you have failed to take sin seriously in your life? How has that affected your walk with God?
- How has your ignorance of sins, big and small, contributed to a feeling of disconnection with God?
- How does a concern for sin differ from a Pharisaic legalism?

Resources

- I highly recommend meditating on 1 John 1. There are some powerful applications to the life of a Christian. What struck me is just how pointed John is with believers, trying to get them to notice their own sin and stop pretending as if they are right in every situation.
- I would also highly recommend meditating on Hebrews 12. I'm struck by the love of God in pursuing sin in our lives as a function of His love. God's love is tough, but true. He refuses to allow His children to dwell in defeat.
- Jerry Bridges has written a powerful book, *Acceptable Sins*. It's a good read on those pesky "OK" sins that often plague Christians.

- Psalm 66
- Isaiah 59
- Romans 6–8
- 1 John 1
- Hebrews 12

iFaith

friend me
Face-to-Face Friendship in a Digital World

We could rephrase the words of Proverbs 24:33–34 about the sluggard and say, "A little Web surfing, a little Facebook, a little folding of the hands around the Smart Phone, and spiritual poverty will come upon you like a robber."
—Josh Harris

We've spent nine chapters exploring faith and intimacy with God in the twenty-first century. For the last chapter, I'd like to explore practical ways twenty-first-century believers can grow closer to God. I purposely put this chapter in the back, because the nature of Christians is to look for a list and ignore the deeper questions of the heart. Lists are the easy way out, but it is the theology we often sidestep that matters most.

Therefore, these practical thoughts are merely an outgrowth of what we believe.

Got that? So if you've skipped ahead, go back and read chapters 1–9. If not, then let's proceed.

The question is, how do we harness emerging technology without becoming its slave?

1. Pursue Genuine Intimacy with God

I think we must pursue genuine intimacy with God by reading His Word, prayer, and walking in the Spirit. Technology has made it easy to be working all the time. As a pastor and author, I often spend hours in front of my computer studying for sermons, working on articles and books, doing business via email, updating Twitter and Facebook.

The truth is all of this may be ministry related and yet it is no substitute for time with God. Unplugged, unbothered, unhindered moments with God. Technology, in many ways, has made it easier to connect in that we have access to the Bible in a variety of media.

Technology has also made it easier to avoid God. There is always another website to check, another Facebook post or Twitter feed to monitors. We can always email, text, or phone friends.

But God speaks and moves among His people just as he did to men of Old. He begs us to draw near and so if we wish to know Him, we must unplug and pursue.

2. Pursue Genuine Intimacy with People

As I write, I have just over 1,000 friends on Facebook. 3,000 people subscribe to my weekly Crosswalk email. I have a few hundred Twitter followers. I have gotten to know and befriend some over the course of the last few years. But digital relationships don't replace flesh-and-blood friendships.

It's easy to fall into the trap of believing that our online life is real life. But Facebook isn't real life. It's a wonderful tool for connecting with a variety of people and can be used for great Kingdom purposes.

But it doesn't replace flesh-and-blood friendships. My advice is to seek times of refreshment and fellowship with good friends, offline. Don't substitute online content for real-life church. Don't substitute a digital chat session for time at the coffee house with a brother in Christ. Don't ignore your real-life family for the seeming approval of your online community.

3. Prioritize Your Technology Choices

Harness technology for your God-given calling rather than letting technology harness you. For every person, technology choices are different. Some view Facebook and Twitter as a waste of time, something that will only detract from their calling. Others such as myself, have found those tools to open great doors of ministry and expand our influence.

I have also found my iPhone to be an invaluable tool, allowing me to have my "office away from the home" and be a source of unlimited podcasts and Christians content that feeds my soul and inspires me in my sermon prep and writing. I also use may websites, online tools, and Bible software.

Each child of God must prayerfully consider what technology you can use and how God wants you to use it. We can easily allow our use of technology to swamp us, to consume all of our time and energy, to rob us of precious time with loved ones and with God.

What works for some may be a waste of time or distraction for others. Ultimately, we should ask ourselves: what saves us time, what expands our influence, what communicates our message?

4. Guard Your Eyes and Heart Online

As advantageous as technology is in equipping us for our God-given calling, it can also be used as a tool of the enemy to lead us into sin. Frankly, knowing our weaknesses, we should set up boundaries with our use of technology.

That might include filters. It should include a level of accountability. And we should avoid extended, meaningful contact with someone of the opposite sex online. Unless its for strict business purposes, I avoid online conversations with women not my wife. I prefer email and always keep my conversation aboveboard.

The threat of unfaithfulness through pornography or online virtual relationships is pervasive. We must run from any temptation that pulls us away from faithfulness to those we're called to love.

5. Give God the Glory with Your Online Presence

I strictly adhere to a policy of "If it's online, it's public." I'm amazed at how free some Christians are in posting swear words, personal information, and dirty jokes on their Facebook profiles or Twitter posts, or on their blogs. Even email should be edited. Because if its digital, if its online, its public.

Imagine your embarrassment if someone read your posts in public or on TV—or in church! We should ask ourselves, *does my online presence glorify God or does it glorify me?*

Because it's so easy to pound out something on the keyboard and post it online, we seem to have forgotten the admonition in James to be *"swift to hear, slow to speak, slow to wrath"* (James 1:19). Large swaths of the Internet are cesspools of gossip, misinformation, crude humor, anger, and half-truths. Sadly, many Christians have taken to the Internet to rant about famous preachers they don't like, private church disputes, and politics. Read the comments on many of the articles on Web sites like *Christianity Today* or *World Magazine.* The things people post are often full of hatred and vitriol.

A Christian should be no part of that. We should honor God with all our words, even the typewritten ones. And we should edify our brothers and sisters in the Lord, even those with whom we disagree.

6. Unplug, Unwind, Enjoy the Old

I'm a lover of technology. My wife, on the other hand, hates it. I check my email every 1.2 seconds. She checks it approximately 1.2 years. And while I'm trying to get her into the twenty-first century, I have come to appreciate her desire to get me to unplug and enjoy the nondigital world.

The truth is that we can let technology become our idol. And in doing so we miss God's best. So if you're like me, do yourself a favor. Unplug. Put the phone down. Take out the earbuds. Close the laptop.

And enjoy real life. Take a walk with your family. Breathe in nature. Read a book, enjoy time with your kids, enjoy one dinner not in front of the TV.

From time to time, seek ways you can streamline your dependence on technology and if there are unnecessary weights and drags on your life, eliminate them.

Online Resources at danieldarling.com:

- Listen to Dan's weekly sermon podcast.
- Read Dan's Friday Five Interview: five questions with leading authors, pastors, and Christian leaders.
- Subscribe to Dan's blog.
- Download free reproducible resources.
- Subscribe to Dan's weekly columns for Crosswalk.

Connect with Dan:

On Facebook: Facebook.com/danieldarling
On Twitter: @dandarling

Some of my favorites to follow:

@andreamullins—Andrea Mullins, publisher, director, New Hope Publishers

@prodigaljohn—Jon Acuff, writer of the popular blog, Stuff Christians Like

@pastortullian—Tullian Tchividjian, senior pastor, Coral Ridge Presbyterian Church

@paultripp—Paul David Tripp, gifted pastor, author, and speaker

@randyalcorn—Randy Alcorn, gifted author and speaker

@pastormark—Mark Driscoll, contemporary pastor and church planter

@drmoore—Dr. Russell Moore, author, dean of theology at Southern Baptist Theological Seminary

@trevinwax—Trevin Wax, blogger, author

@challies—Tim Challies, popular blogger, book reviewer, author

@dreasley—Dr. Michael Easley, past president of Moody Bible Institute

@jackngraham—Jack Graham, senior pastor, Prestonwood Baptist Church

@albertmohler—Al Mohler, president, Southern Baptist Theological Seminary